Life As We Know It

James Mitchum Oates

TABLE OF CONTENTS

Introduction

There is a question that has been posed since the beginning of time that no one has yet been truly able to answer. Many great thinkers and idealists have proposed different analyses in attempts to answer the question, but with so many different proposals, how can you prove or disprove one or the other?

What is life?

I myself have inquired and tried to divulge into a workable explanation for this age-old question. In the first book that I published, which was my life story entitled "Life 101 – A True Life Story," I attempted to tackle this question with facts and analyses in hopes of bringing to light my own perspective.

In the introduction, I give a summation of what I think life is or could be and why I think this. I came up with three different alternatives.

The first was the idea that life is a test. Simply put, those who follow God closely and obey His commands and study and grow in His word in the end will receive the reward of Heaven. Those who do the opposite, then the sanction is Hell.

For me personally, growing up into a world where, more often than not, reality can be replaced by illusion, I can remember believing that science and scientific methodologies could answer the unexplainable mysteries of life. It was difficult for me to believe in a God or deity I had never actually seen. The stories I had heard from the Bible were just that to me, exactly – stories.

But then, as I got older and reflected on my life and saw all the strides I had made and as far as I had come as opposed to where I should've been without the guidance of the Lord, I began to see the light and refine my faith. But a reflection on my life alone was not enough to convince me of the reality of the Divine. It took more. Soon, I started witnessing miracles; not just in my life, but in the lives of others as well, that only an all-good and all-powerful being could create.

But then the biggest factor to help show me that God was, in fact real and active in my life was when He actually spoke to me. When he spoke to me, it wasn't physically, whereas he talked to my heart.

And I listened.

Had I not been open and receptive to his message, I would've missed out and certainly wouldn't be where I am today.

Another factor in the introduction in my life story that I discussed that might define life is the decisions we make. I think most people would agree that every action has a reaction, and every decision has a consequence. We are in control of our own decisions. There are some influences as to what we choose or decide upon, but in the end, it comes down to us as the individual. Some decisions have lesser or greater consequences than others. For example, what one may decide to do may have a not so meaningful impact, but opposed to a person who uses a weapon with criminal intent to knowingly and willingly hurt or kill someone else can not only devastate the well-being of the victim, but can also damage the family, community, and others thereby having a huge impact.

Every decision we make effects someone or something else in some way. This is a rule of life that no one is immune to.

Finally I proposed that life is a learning process. From the time we are born until the time we die, we are constantly learning things that help define who we are. Now I must say that out of these three ideas, I believe that this idea that life is a learning process holds more tenure to it. The reason is that I believe that with this process, the more you learn, the more equipped you are to make sound decisions that will shape your life to good standards. Thus, in essence, the decision-making process is something that is learned, and also the kinds of decisions we make as well. If you learn what is right and what is wrong for you and others, then you can apply this to your decision-making and thus prove your life rewarding and have merit. Granted, just because you have learned the right and just decisions to choose doesn't always mean they will be as easy to apply. However, in such circumstances where one has a difficult time in actually acting out the right decision, there is always someone who can help. You can turn to people who can help intervene in your life and stop you from making negative decisions. But first, you have to decide to reach out for help.

As for this test we take, we must first learn through the learning process how to follow God and grow in His word. And then we must learn to listen to Him when He is speaking to us so we can be properly guided.

Simply put, I believe that these factors are the essential basis that defines life.

Chapter 1

"Alright class, if you will now take out your coloring books and crayons," Mrs. Huddleston announced to the third graders at Pontiac Elementary School.

We had thirty minutes until lunch, and I couldn't wait. I wasn't particularly that hungry. It's just that I was hopeful that we'd be having my favorite – pizza.

I was concentrated on coloring in my coloring book when I happened to look up, and right there standing at my desk was Anna.

Anna was a girl who pretty much kept to herself and didn't really have any friends.

She stood there looking at me for a few seconds, and I was entranced as well.

"Hi Anna," I politely replied.

"Hi William," she responded.

Then she went back to staring again.

This was awkward, so I said the first thing that popped into my mind.

"Do you want to color with me today?"

"That's why I came over."

There was an empty seat next to me. She sat down and then picked up the red crayon. She didn't waste any time coloring the clown's nose.

"Do you know what's for lunch today?" she nonchalantly asked while still coloring.

"No, but I hope it's pizza."

"You like pizza too? It's my favorite."

"Oh yeah, I love pizza."

"Hey, do you want to come to my house for dinner tonight? We're having pizza. You can meet my parents."

I was frozen.

That's very odd. Why is this girl, whom I've hardly ever talked to, inviting me over to her house for pizza? And what's more, why does she want me to meet her parents?

Without further thought, I announced, "I'd love to come to your house."

Then the bell rang for lunch.

Everyday when the bell rings for lunch, I always make sure I'm the last one out. For no particular reason, so I do it on purpose. I always move slower when putting my things away to ensure I'm the last one out.

This day was no different, except when all of the other students had gone and I was then leaving, I saw Anna standing at the door – waiting on me.

Before I could say anything, she announced, "I was hoping we could eat lunch together."

My mind was telling me to say, "No thanks, because I always eat lunch by myself."

But then my heart piped up and I responded, "Sure. That sounds nice."

At lunch, sure enough, we had pizza.

Oh, it was good!

The only problem was that if I were having pizza for dinner at Anna's house and also pizza for lunch, that might be a bit much.

Then I thought to myself, "You're over-thinking it. Pizza for lunch and then dinner. It's fine."

While we ate lunch, right there in the cafeteria, there was an unspoken agreement that we had become friends.

I couldn't wait to meet her parents!

Chapter 2

"In any event, remember to smile and say, 'Yes ma'am, yes sir, no ma'am, no sir when addressing her parents," I thought to myself while sitting on my bed in my room. Mom and dad had already given their approval that I could go to Anna's house for dinner.

I began to imagine what her house looked like. It's probably big with lots of expensive things because her family might be rich. I thought that just from viewing Anna's behavior in class. She's always very shy and quiet. People with a lot of money don't need to interact with others a lot.

My bedroom door was open a little. Dad then stuck his head through.

"You 'bout ready, Will?"

"Yeah, I guess."

The truth was, I was very nervous.

Then he was gone.

Suddenly, I heard a voice in my mind tell me to just lay down and take a nap.

But I couldn't do that.

I had parents to meet and pizza to eat.

So I hopped up and headed for the door.

When we got to the car, I reached in my pocket and pulled out the address she had written down for me on a piece of paper. I then got in the car and read it off to dad so he could know where we were going. I fastened my seatbelt, then noticed my breathing was off a little. This is when I closed my eyes and inhaled slowly through my nose, then exhaled slowly through my mouth.

I did this as sort of a calming effect. Whereas it was supposed to relax me, it did this and a little more. Because I had my eyes closed and the steady rhythm of breathing, it put me to sleep. Before long, I found mom shaking my knee, "Will, wake up. We're here."

I didn't know meditation could be so powerful.

Or maybe I was just more tired than I thought.

I mumbled a few words of confidence, then got out of the car refreshed and ready to meet Anna's parents.

The first thing I noticed was how huge the house was.

It kind-of resembled one of the creepy houses in a Stephen King movie. Then we began to walk up the stairs to the door.

Dad rang the bell and we waited a few seconds. Then a few seconds became longer and then longer. He was about to ring the bell again when the knob began to turn.

When the door finally did open, there stood a man – a rather tall man. And next to him stood a woman who was obviously his wife, but who looked very much younger than to be his wife.

There was a brief silence for a second or two.

Dad then announced, "Hi, we're William's parents," extending his hand to shake the tall man's hand.

The lady then turned her head around and called out, "Anna, William is here."

My dad and the other man had already shaken hands when my mom reached out her hand to shake the other lady's hand.

"I'm Dennis," my dad replied.

"Nice meeting you. I'm Fred."

"And I'm Patricia," my mom very politely exclaimed.

"I'm Ella. Nice meeting you."

"Right this way," Fred said, gesturing with his hand, inviting us in.

As soon as we got in, Ella looked at me and smiled and very charmingly said, "You must be William."

"Yes, ma'am," I responded.

Suddenly, Anna came running up to me and, much to my surprise, grabbed me by the hand.

"The pizza's not here yet, so I figured we'd go to my room until it gets here."

"O.K.," I agreed, and then we went down the hall to Anna's room.

The last thing I heard before we reached Anna's room was Fred reply, "Might we offer you something to drink?"

When we walked into her room, I took in the spacious and lavishness of this one room.

How did the other rooms look?

There were posters on her walls and she had all kinds of trinkets and gadgets that I could only dream of having.

She had carpet on her floor that looked to have been very expensive.

And talk about clean!

Everything was tidy and neatly arranged and organized. Then I remembered how I left my room and how it's been for the past month – a complete mess.

I jokingly thought to myself, "If my parents could see her room in comparison to my room, they might want to trade children."

"Thanks for coming over," Anna piped up.

"Thanks for inviting me. Your mom and dad seem real nice," I lied.

"Yeah, they're pretty cool – sometimes."

"Do you have any brothers or sisters?"

When I asked this, she walked over to her nice, made-up bed and sat down, and then sadly looked at the floor.

"I had a little brother," she lowly replied. "But he died two years ago."

"Oh no," I remorsefully said. "I'm sorry to hear that. If you don't mind me asking, how'd he die?"

Suddenly, a knock at the door.

"Hey guys, the pizza's here," Ella called out.

Then we both hopped up and headed to eat.

"It's this way," Anna announced, leading me to the kitchen as my mouth began to water.

When we got there, Anna's parents were standing there, and the Pizza Hut boxes were on the table with plates as well.

But my parents weren't there.

I felt a cold chill run down my spine as I asked, "Where's my mom and dad?"

Fred then replied, "They had some business to take care of. They'll be here to get you when they're done."

Then that cold chill began to mix with a tingling sensation that gave me a very eerie feeling.

The reason was that when I told them about me coming to Anna's house, they were just as excited as me about the notion of pizza.

But now they're not here and they didn't even say good-bye.

Chapter 3

We ate in silence and had Pepsi to drink. This non-communication while eating was new to me and lasted about twenty minutes or so. The whole time we ate, I struggled to think of something to say or talk about.

Finally, I felt a great sigh of relief when I heard the doorbell ring.

I knew it was them.

Right in the middle of finishing the crust off of a piece, without hesitation, I stood up and remarked, "Thank you all for a great evening. The pizza was really good. Anna, I'll see you at school."

Then I turned around and quickly marched down the hall to the front door. When I got there, I turned the knob.

But the door didn't open. I kept turning and turning the knob. It still didn't open. Then the bell rang again.

"Mom, dad!" I began to whine as I frantically turned the knob over and over.

Suddenly I felt a hand on my shoulder. I nearly broke my neck when I jerked it around so hard to face them.

"Are you alright?" Fred asked in a very mellow tone.

"Yeah," I nervously replied. "I'm just trying to get the door open."

He then responded, "The door was locked," then twisted the latch underneath it.

I turned and twisted the knob, and it flew open.

And there stood my parents.

I embraced them both in a big hug, but careful not to cry because I could feel Anna and her parents' eyes on me.

"Did you have a good time?" dad asked.

"Oh, I missed both of you so much."

"William, honey, we weren't gone very long," mom replied.

"Can we go home now?" I asked. "I think I ate too much pizza and I'd like to lay down."

Mom then gave dad a puzzled look and responded, "Sure."

Dad then directed his attention to the family standing at the door.

"Thank you for having William over," he said extending his hand to shake Fred's.

"It was our pleasure," Fred replied, shaking dad's hand.

Something in Fred's voice when he said this gave me that same chill as before.

Then we headed for the car. When we got to the car, I turned to see them still standing there in the doorway – watching. I waved to Anna, and she slowly waved back. It wasn't until we got in the car that they finally closed the door.

Then we drove home.

The more distance we put between them and us on the way home, the better I felt.

We were all silent until we got there.

When we finally got in the house, is when I decided to let it all out.

"Mom, dad, what's the big idea leaving me alone in a strange house with strange people? And what's more, you didn't even tell me you were leaving. I was scared to death."

"William, calm down," dad piped up. "We thought you were

looking forward to this. You know what, son, I think Anna likes you," he said on a milder note.

"Likes me? Of course, she likes me – for now. This is the way it starts out in all the horror movies."

"Honey, don't you think you're over-reacting?" mom chimed in.

"No, I was scared as hell!"

"Alright, that's enough, young man. You'll not use that kind of language in this household. Go to your room right now," dad replied.

I marched off to my room. When I got in and closed the door, I layed on my bed and stared at the ceiling in deep thought.

In my mind, I pondered dad's words, "You know what, son, I think Anna likes you."

Here was a problem because I knew she liked me, and now she would want to hang out with me more often. Which also meant she would invite me back to her creepy house with her creepy parents. I can't tell her no because I don't have an excuse for not wanting to go.

Oh, the price for being charming!

Chapter 4

As expected, Anna took it upon herself to get closer and more involved with me despite the lack of interest I showed in her. We ate together in the cafeteria, played together at recess, and yes, I went to her house more often.

She thought we were becoming good friends.

I looked at it as a burden.

Every time I went to her house, I would spend the majority of the visit in her room because I didn't want to be around her creepy parents. The way they were always so silent and meek made me think they had something to hide.

Then Anna invited me to her birthday party. And what date was she born?

October 30, the day before Halloween.

Aw, hell no!

She caught me off guard when she asked me to come, so like

always, I said yes.

Against my better judgement.

She gave out invitations a week in advance. So that gave me a good amount of time to think of an excuse as to why I couldn't go.

Finally after days of serious contemplation over a plausible excuse, I found myself frustrated because I couldn't think of a good reason to opt out.

Whatever lie I could think of would be an obvious ploy for avoidance.

Before I knew it, it was time.

There I sat on my bed thinking hard for this last minute chance.

Then I thought, "If I were to say I was sick, it might work if I had my parents to verify it for me. I can't just tell them I'm sick. I have to show them. And what better way to do that than vomiting?"

So I hopped up and raced to the bathroom. As soon as I got there, I closed the door and leaned over the toilet. Then I stuck my finger in my mouth and back towards my throat.

Nothing.

So I went deeper.

Still nothing.

Then I told myself, "It's either you vomit or go to this party and get super spooked out."

So I went even deeper.

Finally I began to gag and there it came.

I vomited.

When I was done, I surveyed my work in the toilet.

"Mission accomplished," I said.

Then I left the bathroom holding my stomach and leaning over as if to appear in dire need.

Then I saw dad coming down the hall. He saw me all bent over and replied, "Will, what's wrong?"

"I don't feel too good. I just threw up," I weakly responded.

Then mom came down the hall.

"What's going on? Will, are you ready?"

"He's not feeling O.K. He just threw up," dad replied.

Then they both looked at each other and the looks on their faces was of a little bit of amusement.

Did they think this was funny?

"Well, we'll probably have to take him to the hospital. I don't know what they'll give him," mom said.

"Oh, they'll probably give him a shot," dad replied. "And then who knows how long he'll be there; could be weeks."

This is when I piped up, "You know, I think I threw up because of this new candy I tried. But I'm feeling much better now."

"So does that mean you're ready to go?" mom inquired.

"Yeah, definitely," I hurriedly responded.

Then we made our way to the car and was on our way to Anna's house.

Chapter 5

I expected the worst while being there. But surprisingly enough, I had a pretty good time. I didn't think I'd ever loosen up around Anna to the point where I would dance around her – ever. But in no time at all, there I was doing my best moves to the songs on the stereo. We ate and talked, and suddenly things weren't so scary.

I saw a few people from class, but I didn't talk to them. I only interacted with Anna.

Then came the part when she was to open her gifts.

Just seeing the gifts she was receiving from other peers put me to shame when I thought about what I got her.

Then she got to my gift.

I so badly wanted to save myself the embarrassment that I would feel when she opened my gift, and try to somehow stop her from opening it.

But it was too late.

There she held it in her hands.

A birthday card, and when she opened it, five dollars fell onto the floor. She picked the five dollars up and then silently began to read the card.

As she read, I could detect something in her eyes. It was of strong emotions that I could not place or identify. But one emotion that I definitely sensed was admiration.

Then, when she was done reading the card, she walked over to me and very gently hugged me.

I wondered why is she fascinated with this mediocre gift. It certainly wasn't anything in comparison to the other gifts.

It wasn't until later that night, after the party was over and everyone had left, that it hit me.

There lying in my bed thinking about what a wonderful time I had, I began to ponder upon why she obviously liked my poor gift so much; and even enough to give me a hug.

I then knew it wasn't the quality of the gift that she cared so much for, but for the simple fact that it was from me.

After that night, Anna and I grew closer and closer. I was still somewhat leery of her parents, but after a while, I got used to being around them. So much so that Anna's house soon became my home away from home.

Although I still felt that certain chill whenever entering her house.

Not only that, but our parents became good friends with one another as well. Anna's parents treated me like a son, and my parents treated her like a daughter. We had lots of family outings together, and life was good.

Before we knew it, it was time to go to the next school grade.

We were best friends in the fourth grade as well. We shared secrets with each other and just enjoyed being around each other.

Our relationship was steadily blossoming and growing.

We went through fourth grade, then fifth grade, then sixth grade together. But when we hit seventh grade, that's when certain changes started to take place for both of us.

Then one day, I was in my room lying in bed staring at the ceiling thinking about Anna, when I heard a knock at my door.

"Who is it?" I asked.

"It's me," dad replied.

"Who is me? That could be anyone," I jokingly inquired.

"Ha, ha, you're a great comedian," dad chimed. "Can I come in?"

"Sure."

Dad came in and closed the door behind him.

"Can we talk for a minute, son?" he seriously asked.

"Yeah," I said sitting up. "What's up?"

"Well I think it's time we have that talk. I know you're going through changes as a young man, and that's natural."

He then told me the entire story of the birds and the bees and how Mother Nature works.

I listened, but not with great interest because most of it I already knew.

"Dad, what's the purpose of this talk?"

"Just think about what I said," dad interrupted.

Then he stood up and walked to the door. When he got to the door, he stopped and, without turning around, he announced, "And dinner will be ready in fifteen minutes."

Then he walked out.

Chapter 6

"Thanks for helping me with my homework, William. Because of you, I got a "B plus" on my quiz," Anna said as we stood out in the hallway in between classes.

Then she reached over and embraced me in a hug.

There we stood looking at each other for a few seconds in silence. My thoughts were racing a mile a minute, and I felt as if my heart was about to hop out of my chest from beating so fast.

"Anna, there's something I want to tell you."

Then the bell rang for the next class to start.

"Can it wait until after school today?"

Although she knew it couldn't.

"Yeah, sure," I piped up.

"O.K., see you after school."

"Alright."

With that, she turned and walked to her class.

As she walked away, there I stood, entranced, staring at her. I knew she could feel my eyes upon her.

Then she disappeared in the crowd.

I then turned and headed for my class.

Oh, how I longed for 3:00 p.m. to get here!

In class, I couldn't focus on what the teacher was saying. I was in deep thought of Anna and how to compose the right words to say to her.

Then I felt a tap on my shoulder. I looked behind me to see Diane Chandler handing me a folded up piece of paper. I took it, turned back around and unfolded it. Then I began to read, "My dear sweet William."

I read the entire love letter, and when I got to the end, it read, "Yours forever, Diane."

Any normal boy would've been overjoyed and ecstatic to receive a love letter from Diane. She was very pretty and popular.

If she would've given the letter to any other guy in class, they would've fallen at her feet.

But not me.

I felt as if I were already taken.

Right there, I tore the note up into shreds.

"What the hell?" I heard her exclaim from behind me.

"You'll never get another chance," I heard her wickedly reply.

But I didn't care. I was proud of my decision.

Then the bell rang for the next class.

The rest of the school day, I tried to focus and pay attention in class.

But to no avail.

All I could think about was Anna and the way she walked and the way she talked and the way she smiled.

I couldn't take it anymore.

Finally, the bell rang to go home.

I gathered my stuff and quickly made my way out the door.

I arrived at the same place where we talked earlier this morning in hopes that she would meet me here.

Soon, I began to get anxious and paranoid that she wouldn't even show up.

"Patience, Will, it's only been six minutes since the bell rang," I said to myself.

Suddenly I heard her sweet voice call my name.

I turned to see her standing there.

"Thank God you came. I was starting to think you weren't going to show," I anxiously exclaimed.

"Will, what's wrong?" she concernedly asked.

"Well, I was just wondering if, you know, well if you wouldn't mind..."

"Just say it, Will."

"Will you be my girlfriend?" I asked in a half-whisper.

Then I so badly wanted to lean in and kiss her on the mouth.

Much to my surprise, she leaned in and kissed me and then replied, "I thought you'd never ask."

Chapter 7

Anna and I decided to keep our relationship a secret from everyone – even our parents.

But we both kind-of suspected that somehow they knew.

I felt that at this point, I would do anything for Anna, including fight tooth and nail for her – literally.

One day at recess, Anna and I were playing together like we normally do, when Tom Hemford and his buddies approached us. I already didn't like Tom to begin with, so when he began picking and taunting me and Anna, this really ticked me off.

"Look at the two lovebirds. I wonder if their children will be just as weird as they are."

Then they began laughing.

I bald my fist up ready for a fight. This is when Anna grabbed my arm and stopped me from advancing.

"Will, don't," she replied.

I took Anna by the hand and we walked away. The look I threw at Tom let him know not to follow us.

That look said it all.

We finally found a spot in the shade underneath a tree to just chill.

There we sat. I was in deep thought trying to think of something to say.

Finally I retorted, "I don't know why Tom is so mean."

"That's just the way people are. Maybe he's jealous."

"Maybe so."

Then the teacher started calling the students in because recess was over.

"Hey, can I come over today after school?" I said standing up.

"Yeah, sure," she replied.

The rest of the school period, I focused and paid attention in class. Normally in class, I would be distracted by something else or just not listening to the teacher. But for some reason today, I was alert, participated in class, and actually learned a few things.

Before long, the bell rang to go home.

I decided to hang out on the school grounds for a few minutes longer to stay with my buddies. As we sat on the bench outside, we talked and laughed for a little bit until Roger asked me what's going on between me and Anna.

This is when I got a confident aire and began to brag about how Anna was my girlfriend. Only my aire was a little too confident.

I looked at my watch and twenty minutes had passed and I figured I'd better head to Anna's.

"Alright guys, later," I said, beginning the journey to Anna's house.

"Later," they responded.

As I walked, I thought about this desire I had for the last few days - chocolate ice-cream.

"Maybe Anna will have some when I get there," I thought to myself.

In no time at all, I was there.

I knocked on the door, and a few seconds later, it opened.

There stood Anna.

"Come on in," she said.

As I walked in, I replied, "First and foremost do you have any chocolate ice-cream?"

"Yeah," she said, and then led me to the kitchen.

When we got to the kitchen, she opened the freezer and pulled out a box of chocolate ice-cream. We then dished up our bowls and indulged. When we were done is when she decided she wanted to play video games in her room. When we got to her room, she popped in the Shinobi cartridge in her game system. There we both sat, very full and having fun.

But then I got serious for a moment.

I turned to her and asked her exactly what did happen to her little brother.

She fixed a very odd look at me.

"I remember the first day I came over to your house, we were talking about it. You started to tell me how he died, but you never finished."

I'd rather not tell."

"Please. It can't be that bad, is it?"

"Actually it is."

"Alright, if you'd rather not talk about it, that's fine."

34

"O.K., I'll tell you. My little brother's name was Adam. He was born with lung complications and was here at home. One day, my parents were in the front yard preparing for the Easter egg hunt for Easter. I walked over to his crib and picked him up. I just wanted to hold him. But then I accidentally dropped him. I ran to the front yard and in a frenzy told them what happened. We rushed Adam to the hospital, but it was too late. When we got there, they told us he was dead. As soon as the doctors told us this, I looked at my parents for a response. But the look in their eyes said it all. It was a very distant but odd look. And since then, things have never been the same."

"I'm sorry to hear that," I replied.

Then Anna began to sniffle. "It always hurts remembering that. I can see it like it was yesterday."

Then I looked at my watch. "Anna, I'd better be going," I announced. "I promised my mom and dad I'd help them with something."

By this time Anna was really crying.

I didn't really promise to help mom and dad with anything. I just wanted to give Anna her space so she can grieve.

Chapter 8

When I got home, dad was sitting on the front porch reading a magazine.

"Hey, dad," I replied.

"Hey Will," he responded, still reading his magazine. "How was school today?"

"Oh, same ole, same ole. Just trying to stay out of trouble."

Then he looked up from the magazine and directly at me. The look on his face was odd. It was a look of proudness.

But what was he proud of?

"Alright, son. Dinner should be ready in an hour."

"O.K."

Then I walked into the house and went to my room.

And so for years, Anna and I went as boyfriend and girlfriend. We entered high school together and were the cutest couple. We went to the movies together, out shopping, and our favorite thing was going to Peter Piper's Pizzeria on Friday's.

We were inseparable.

When we'd talk on the phone to each other at night, we'd both end our conversation with, "I love you."

We went all four years through high school together. Then came the big day – graduation.

I was never so nervous in all my life. While I was in my room getting dressed, dad came in and gave me his pep talk. Two minutes after he left, mom came in and remarked on how handsome I looked. Then, as she straightened my tie, she suddenly burst into tears.

"Mom, don't cry," I soothingly said.

"I'm sorry, honey. It's just that I finally get to see the day my boy becomes a man."

Then we embraced in a hug.

"I love you, mom."

"I love you, too, Will," she replied, sniffling.

Dad then opened the door and stuck his head in.

"Come on, we don't want to be late," he announced.

Mom then looked at dad and, with tears in her eyes, remarked, "Look at our boy all grown up."

Then dad came in and we all embraced in one big hug.

"I'm proud of you, son," dad said.

Then he looked at his watch and teasingly replied, "I'd be even prouder of you if you actually graduate."

"O.K., give me a second."

"Alright, babe," mom responded.

Then they turned and left.

I splashed on some Aqua Velva cologne and combed my hair. There I stood and looked in the mirror for a moment.

"You did it," I said to myself in a whisper.

Then I was ready to graduate.

When I got there, I looked to see if I could see Anna.

But I didn't, so I just waited patiently.

I really wanted to talk to her.

Then it began.

The speeches were given, and before long, the names of the graduating class of 1998 were being called one by one to accept their diploma. Finally, Anna's name was called and I cheered so loudly, I almost got hoarse. Soon, my name was called. As I walked across the stage, I could hear the loud cheers for me.

And soon enough, just like that, it was over.

I met up with mom and dad and we decided to go out to eat.

We went to Applebee's.

When we got there, a waiter showed us to our table. When we were seated, I asked, "Shouldn't Anna be here too?"

Dad then put a smile on his face and replied, "Oh, I'm sure you and Anna will catch up later."

The night rolled on, and as we ate, we talked. We talked about me finding a job and possibly going to college. Finally, we were done and headed home.

When we got home, it was 11:30 p.m. I put my pajamas on and climbed in bed and stared at the ceiling – waiting.

But what was I waiting on?

Finally, at 1:02 a.m., the phone rang.

"Hello."

"Hi Will."

"Oh, hi Anna."

"You can come on over."

"Alright, I'll be there soon."

"Alright, bye."

"Bye."

Then I hopped up and threw my clothes on. I slowly walked through the house, careful to not make a sound, and then made my way to the back door because the back door is a lot quieter than the front.

When I got out, I made my way to Anna's house.

Finally, I arrived. I had enough sense to go around to the back door. A minute later, the door opened. There was Anna. She put her finger to her lips, letting me know to be quiet. Slowly, we made our way through the house and to her bedroom. When we got there, she closed the door behind us.

"Are you sure this is what you want?" I asked.

"I've waited for this my whole life. Now turn off the light."

Chapter 9

What Anna and I did remained a secret. We never told anyone. This was our first time going all the way. It was an experience neither of us would ever forget.

As for me, it made me feel like I was at the height of my manhood.

And it showed like never before. I started taking on challenges and obstacles just to prove to myself that now I was a real man.

I was having the time of my life.

Although my graduation would've been really great had mom and dad bought me better gifts. Then one day, I went to the bakery to get donuts for us all at dad's request. I didn't really feel like going, and I just wanted to be at home today. But dad urged and urged so finally I went. The donut shop was a few blocks away, so with money in my pocket, I began the journey. As I walked, the coolness of the air whisked by gently striking my face, putting me in an even more calm mood.

I began to think – about everything. I remembered how I first met Anna when we were kids, and how my first impression of her was not good. Then we got closer and closer to each other, and soon how that impression changed. Then I remembered our first kiss. Then, finally what happened on graduation night.

Before long, I was at the bakery.

I walked in and there to greet me was the aroma of freshly baked donuts. I walked up to the counter and a middle-aged, heavy-set, bald man was there to greet me. I ordered the donuts, paid the man, and left.

As I walked home, I felt that same gentle breeze once again.

Then something hit me.

Maybe Anna and I did something wrong by having sex. It certainly felt right, but did we violate our parents' trust? We almost made that mistake when we were younger.

But we didn't.

Maybe we should tell them what we did. They probably would be very understanding, seeing as we're older now.

Right then and there, I decided that when I got home, I would have this discussion with mom and dad.

As I walked, my hands got clammy just from the idea of what dad might say. And then to make things worse, what would Anna's parents say?

Just thinking about the stern words that might resonate from Anna's father sent a chill up my spine.

But nonetheless, it had to be done.

Before I knew it, I was almost home.

When I got half a block away from the house, I thought to myself, "We must have company."

The reason I thought that was because I saw a car parked in front of the house that wasn't there when I left.

Then I said to myself, "Whoever this is is some kind of high roller." And that was because the make of the car appeared to be expensive, and the color was cherry red.

Then I was home.

There I stood admiring this gem of a beauty when I heard dad pipe up and say, "Well, are you just gonna stare at it or take it for a spin?"

I couldn't believe what he just said. My eyes began to water, and then I started coughing from getting choked up by my own tears.

"Dad, it's beautiful!" I exclaimed.

He then began to walk towards me and then stopped some feet away. He tossed me the keys and said, "Go on. Have a good time."

I ran to him and gave him a hug. I embraced him for a few seconds before I realized I was smashing the donuts.

"Thanks dad. You're the greatest," I said, handing him the crushed donuts.

I ran to the car, hopped in, and started it up.

"Don't be out too late," he replied.

Then I was gone.

I was headed straight to Anna's house.

When I got there, I pulled up front and honked the horn. About a minute later, the door opened, and there stood the love of my life.

"Oh my God!" she exclaimed and began to run towards the car.

"Is this yours?" she excitedly asked.

"I'm as surprised as you are. Hop in, let's go for a ride."

"Alright," she said, getting in.

When she got in and closed the door, I suddenly heard Anna's dad reply, "Have fun, you two."

"Thanks, Mr. Fielding," I responded while waving to him.

Then we were gone.

Where I was driving to, I had no idea.

I drove and drove and we talked about everything. The sun was just starting to set when I asked Anna to look in the glove department for the manual. She opened it and when she did, out fell some packs of condoms.

"Will, look at this," she excitedly exclaimed.

"Dad, you really are the greatest," I said out loud.

"Well looks like I know where we're headed now," she said placing her hand on my knee.

I knew where we were headed, too. There was a hill in the city limits that we often went to that overlooked the entire city.

COUSIN JOEY

Chapter 10

"Yeah, so I was thinking about Northwestern University in Chicago, IL.," I excitedly said to Anna.

We were at my house in my room, sitting down on the bed, discussing possible colleges we might want to attend. We both did well on our SAT's and ACT's and were accepted at many. But one thing we decided on, we definitely wanted to go to the same one so we could be together.

"Well, I kind of like the idea of Park University in Parkville, MO.," she exclaimed.

Then a knock at the door.

"Come in," I replied.

Dad came in and announced, "Will, I'd like to speak to you for a moment."

"Sure," I said, waiting for him to speak.

"In private," he retorted. "Excuse us, Anna."

He then turned to leave. I looked at Anna and quizzically shrugged my shoulders because I didn't know what it was that was so important he wanted to talk to me about, and why he was so serious.

I hoped everything was alright.

So when we got down the hall, I asked him, "Is everything alright?"

"Walk with me for a minute, son," he said, not looking at me.

We walked in silence until we got to the front porch. Finally, he replied, "Have a seat." And then he sat down as well.

"What's going on, dad?"

"Well, Will, I know that you and Anna are planning to go away to college together, and that's great. That's why it pains me to ask you if maybe you could postpone your plans – just for a little while."

"Well, how long? Why?"

"Your cousin Joey is coming to town and he wants to spend some quality time specifically with you."

"Cousin Joey?"

"Yeah, you might not remember him, but he came to your fifteenth birthday party."

"I vaguely remember him. I don't understand why this has to interfere with me and Anna's college plans."

"He wants to spend some time with you; so that you two can hang out and bond together."

"But why me? How long?"

"He asked to spend time with you specifically. It'll only be for a year or so."

"But why should I put my life on hold because a cousin, whom I hardly know, wants to be buddies all of a sudden?"

"His mom and dad both recently died, Will. They were killed in a car accident, and now he just needs comfort."

"I'm sorry to hear that," I quietly said, looking down.

"It'll only be for a little while, and then you can get back to your regular life."

My better judgement told me to say, "No,"and then make plans with Anna to leave as soon as possible.

But because of my strong self-restraint, against my better judgement, I said, "O.K."

"Thanks, Will," dad said with a half-smile on his face.

"Well, let me go tell Anna the change of plans."

I stood up and walked into the house while dad sat there staring out into the world.

When I got to my room, there was Anna sitting on the bed waiting.

"Well, Anna, looks like there's been a change of plans. You see, my cousin Joey..."

Before I could say another word, Anna interrupted, "I know. I was at the front door listening. I think it's a wonderful idea for your cousin Joey to stay here for a while. I'm willing to wait on college if you are."

I was shocked.

Why was she so willing to put our entire future on hold?

I thought that was odd.

Chapter 11

I tried to get everything ready so as to make Joey's stay comfortable and easy.

Finally, the day came when he would arrive. He was to come by train and we were supposed to meet him at the station.

Who uses the train anymore?

Anna insisted on coming.

It was a long ride from our house to the train station. And the whole time we rode, there was silence. I didn't know what to expect and I didn't have anything to say. Part of the reason for this silence on my part was due to an eerie, gut-wrenching feeling I had while we rode. It very much so reminded me of the same spine-tingling chill I had when I first met Anna's parents.

Finally, we arrived at the station.

We were on time and waited in the area he said he would meet us at. After about fifteen minutes, I retorted, "Remind me why I'm doing this now."

"It's too late to back out now, son," dad half-heartedly replied.

Two minutes later, approaching us was a young man about my age wearing denim jeans and a faded gray shirt. As I looked more carefully, the closer he got, the more I could see how handsome he was.

Soon, he was right in front of us.

Then dad announced, "Will, you remember your cousin Joey?"

I looked at dad for a moment. I wanted to tell him, "No, I don't remember him," and then take Anna by the hand and go get ready to leave for college.

I looked away from dad and fixed my eyes upon Anna, who was staring at Joey. Then I looked at him, and he had his gaze on her as well.

I purposely coughed to disrupt this brief encounter. When I did, Anna quickly looked at me and then back to him, and then she looked down.

I then looked at Joey, and he tried to play it off as well.

"Can I get your bags for you?" dad interrupted.

"No, no," Joey replied. "Thanks, but I got it."

"Will, you haven't even said hello yet," dad hastened.

"Oh hi, Joey," I announced as if snapping out of a trance. "How long's it been?"

"Oh, it's been a while. We've got so much to catch up on."

"Will, aren't you going to introduce me?" Anna replied.

"Oh, I'm sorry. Anna, this is my cousin, Joey. Joey, this is my girlfriend, Anna. I must've forgot."

But I didn't forget. I was trying to avoid it for as long as possible.

"Nice meeting you," Anna softly said and extending her hand.

"And you as well," Joey responded in a mellow tone, extending his hand also.

Only I thought his tone was too mellow.

"Well, we should be going," dad piped up. "I hope you're hungry."

"Oh, I'm starved."

With that, we headed home.

Chapter 12

Much to my chagrin, Joey's time with us was actually somewhat pleasant. It wasn't as much of a pain as I thought it would be. We did some bonding and lots of "guy" stuff. We played football with each other and liked to watch boxing. We had more in common than I could imagine.

On this particular day, we just tossed the football back and forth to each other in the front yard while dad sat on the porch reading a magazine.

"That game was amazing!" I announced. "That was by far the greatest Super Bowl I've ever seen."

"Yeah, that was a pretty good game. But still, I wanted the Falcons to win."

"I'm just glad my team won. I've always been a huge Broncos fan."

"Go long," Joey announced.

I ran long and fast, and then Joey launched a perfect spiral, and I caught it.

"Yay! Touchdown Broncos! Elway does it again," I yelled.

Then I began to sprint to him for celebration. When I got to him, I replied, "How about another one?"

He then lowly responded, "Actually I'm starting to feel kind-of tired. I think I'll take a quick nap."

"O.K. sure," I said, glancing over at dad who was looking at me.

Joey then went into the house.

A few seconds after Joey had gone in, dad said, "Come on up and talk to me for a moment."

I walked up the stairs not knowing what he wanted to talk about.

"Sit, sit," he replied, motioning to the chair next to him.

"How do you like your cousin coming to stay with us?" he said, not looking at me.

"It's been O.K."

"Has he been alright?" he asked, turning the page in his

magazine.

"Actually, I'm enjoying his company very much. We have a lot in common."

"As long as you're happy, son," he said, turning to look me directly in the eyes.

But his look was a peculiar one. It was somewhat distant.

Then Anna came to the front door.

"Will, can I talk to you for a minute?" she announced.

"Sure," I said, standing up and walking past dad to go into the house.

He went back to reading his magazine.

"What's up, babe?" I exclaimed.

"Come on," she said, motioning with her hand. "The walls have ears."

We walked past Joey's room and to my room. When we got there, she closed the door behind us.

"Is everything O.K.?"

"It's time we talk."

"I'm listening."

"Well, I get the distinct notion that maybe Joey might need to stay a little longer than planned."

"Why do you say that?"

"He seems so down and depressed from losing Eddie and Tiffany, and it's obviously taking a huge toll on him. But when he's with you, he's much happier and in good spirits."

"Wait, how did you know his parents' names? I never told you."

"We talked while you went to the store yesterday."

"What else have you two talked about?"

Even though I didn't say this out loud and was just thinking it, I knew that Anna knew this question was on my mind.

Chapter 13

All of my life, I always had somewhat of a problem when it came to listening to my better judgement. When Anna told me she thought Joey should stay longer, my instinct told me to wish Joey luck in the future, thank mom and dad for all of their support and being my parents, and catch the next flight to Berkeley, California, to start college with or without Anna.

But instead, once again, I gave in to the pressure and acted out of a feeling of what someone else wanted.

Joey ended up staying longer than planned.

Whereas at first I had the notion that Joey and I were bonding very well and that I actually liked him being around, soon enough I began to realize that this was just a false illusion.

I started to loathe his company and couldn't wait until he left. Not only was his mere presence beginning to irritate me, but I also hated having Anna around him.

The way he would look at her very often on several occasions almost drove me to address the issue to him.

But I didn't.

Once again, this was me not listening to my better judgement.

But then on Thanksgiving, something happened that almost really made me lose my cool.

Anna, Joey, and me were on the front porch talking while mom and dad worked frivolously to prepare the Thanksgiving meal.

"So what college are you guys looking at going to?" Joey asked, directing his attention to me.

"We were undecided and making plans. But all that's been put on hold now," I retorted.

"Will, you are so lucky to have a girl like Anna. I only wish that someday I could have a relationship with somebody and have as good a bond as you two."

"Hmmm," I said to myself under my breath.

"Will, can you come in for a minute?" mom announced from the kitchen.

"On my way," I said, springing up from my chair and heading into the house.

When I walked in, I had to pause for a moment and take in the wonderful aromas of Thanksgiving dinner.

Then I ventured to the kitchen to see mom and dad hard at work.

"Hey mom."

"Oh hey, honey. Listen, do you know where the sage is? You were using it last night."

"Yeah, sure," I said, walking over to the cabinet and moving the box of macaroni out of the way.

"I put it back here," I announced, handing it to her.

"Oh, thanks, honey," she replied.

"Is it almost ready?" I asked, rubbing my stomach.

"In a little bit," she responded.

"Good, cause I'm hungry as a horse," I said, turning to leave.

I walked back to the living room, and the front door was ajar – perfect for spying.

I just stood there and listened.

"So, do you have a girlfriend back home?" Anna asked.

"No, it's been kind-of hard for me to find anyone."

"Why's that?"

"Well, for one, I'm not as handsome as most guys. And certainly not as handsome as Will."

"I don't think you're a bad looking guy. I think you're very handsome."

"Handsome enough to date?"

"Well, if I were single, I would probably get with you."

"Would you?" he responded in a low whisper.

Enough was enough!

"Alright, just what are you trying to pull?" I announced, opening the screen door and stepping out. "That does it. I want you gone."

"Don't worry, Will. I'll be leaving in two days."

But why was he all of a sudden so eager to leave?

Maybe because he knew the damage had already been done.

Chapter 14

As promised, Joey was packed up and ready to leave in two days. He left the same way he came – in a heat of disarray and by train. Anna insisted on coming to bid Joey farewell.

While we were at the station waiting for his train to arrive, I couldn't help but keep constant vigil eyes on both Anna and Joey. I didn't want them looking at each other or even making eye contact.

Almost as if they could feel my eyes upon both of them and could sense the tension that emulated from me, neither one of them looked at the other.

Finally, his train arrived.

"Well, Joey, it was good seeing you again. Take care and don't forget to write," I sarcastically said, obviously trying to hurry him along.

With luggage in hand, Joey replied, "Thanks for having me, Uncle Dennis," speaking to dad.

"It was a pleasure having you," dad responded.

Then he directed his attention to me.

He started to say something, but it just didn't come out. Instead, he piped up and said, "See ya around, Will."

I had a feeling that what he was going to say at first was going to be an apology.

Then he glanced at Anna and lowly said, "Bye."

"Take care of yourself, Joey."

Then he boarded the train.

We watched as he made his way to a seat. He finally found a seat near a window. Then he fixed his eyes upon Anna. I looked at her, and she too was watching him. Slowly, the train began to depart, and the whole time, their gazes were locked. Suddenly, before he disappeared towards his journey home, he put his hand up and waved at her, and she waved back.

It was as if I weren't even there.

And with that, I let out a deep breath. It was a breath of relief. All of those aggressions and jealous feelings went out with that breath.

I felt like we could finally get our lives back on track again.

I began thinking about planning for me and Anna's future as soon as we got home.

I had already forgiven her.

"Well, that's that," I said, trying to hurry us along out of the station.

We turned and left to go home.

Joey was finally out of the picture. And with that reality came a sense of comfort. Now my focus was getting Anna back on board with the original plan.

We rode home in silence.

There was nothing to say.

When we pulled up to the red stop light, Anna announced, "If it's O.K., Mr. Warner, I think I'll be going home now."

"Are you sure? We were all just now heading out to lunch," dad replied.

"I'd love to, but I have a slight headache and I think I need to lie down for a bit."

I looked over at her, and she was just staring out the window. I knew that she knew I was looking at her.

Dad then began the drive to Anna's house.

When we got there, Anna replied, "Thank you, Mr. Warner. Bye, Will. Call me later."

"O.K.," I responded.

Then she got out, and I watched her make the journey to her front door. She put the key in the lock and it opened. Then she disappeared behind the wooden frame.

Finally, we drove home.

When we got there, mom was all ready to go out to eat.

"Hey, I think I'm starting to feel kind-of tired and might need to lie down for a bit. You can go without me," I announced as I made my way to my room.

"Well, just more for us," dad said to mom. "Get some rest. We'll see you in a little bit."

"O.K."

When I got to my room, I nearly dove for the bed – shoes on and all.

I just lay there with my eyes open. About ten minutes later, the phone rang.

I got up to answer it.

"Hello."

"Hi Will."

"Oh, hey Anna."

"Listen, Will, I just want to say I'm sorry for everything."

"Oh, it's water under the bridge. I'm not mad."

"Good, because I hope that you can really try hard to forgive me for what I'm about to tell you."

I suddenly felt a lump in my throat.

"What is it?" I asked.

"One time when Joey and I were alone, we actually kissed."

I was in total shock for a moment.

But why should I have been in shock?

Everyone knew they had something going on the side.

Everyone, including me.

Chapter 15

I decided not to say anything to mom and dad about what Anna did.

I just bottled it up inside me. But then they knew that something wasn't quite right with me. From my withdrawal status to mood swings to less eating, they knew that there was a problem. The way they approached dealing with this was to try to make me forget about whatever it was I was going through and to cheer me up.

This behavior of mine had been going on for a few weeks. Then one day, I was in my room sitting on my bed, sulking until I heard a knock at the door.

"Come in," I exclaimed.

The door opened, and in stepped dad.

"Hey, Will."

"Hey, dad."

"Listen, this afternoon your mom and I are going to the movies and then out to dinner, so get ready."

"If it's O.K., I'd rather stay here."

"But the movie we're going to see is the new one with Chris Tucker."

"Maybe next time."

"But Chris Tucker is your favorite actor."

"Yeah, I'll have to catch it at a later date."

"Alright, what's going on? Your mother and I have been noticing you've been kind-of down lately."

"I really don't want to talk about it."

"How can we help you if we don't know what's going on? You know, if you just get it off your chest, it'll make you feel a lot better."

"O.K., well, Anna and Joey kissed one time."

I looked at dad, and the reaction I expected from him about this news was one of surprisal. But it wasn't that at all. He didn't look a bit surprised, but instead nonchalant and almost as if he were anticipating me saying that.

"Well, this is where you be a man and tell her how you feel about her. If you don't talk to her, you could let her get away."

"But I was so hurt when I heard it. I wouldn't know what to say."

"Exactly. You were hurt. Tell her that so she won't do it again."

"I guess you're right."

After a few seconds of silence, dad announced, "Well, what are you waiting for? Go and get your girl."

"But what else do I say? I don't want her to do anything like that ever again."

"Just listen to your heart. Let it be your guide and you'll be just fine."

"Alright, I'll call her right now."

"It's probably better that you talk to her in person."

With that, dad stood up and headed for the door.

"Wait, where are you going?"

"To catch the movie. Chris Tucker is hilarious."

Then he was gone.

I let out a deep sigh and whispered to myself, "God, give me the strength to do this."

Then I, too headed for the door.

I pulled up in front of Anna's house and just sat there a moment. As I stared at the house, I remembered the creepy, spine-tingling feeling I got when I first saw it.

Then I got out of the car and made my way to the front door.

I rang the doorbell, and when I did, I heard Anna's voice respond, "Who is it?"

Although something was different about her voice. She sounded more jovial and happy.

"It's Will."

A few seconds later, the door flung open, and there she was in tears.

"Oh, Will, I'm so sorry," she exclaimed and then embraced me in a hug.

"It's O.K.," I responded, hugging her as well. "I forgive you. Start getting your things ready. We're leaving for Berkeley, CA, in a week."

Chapter 16

It surprised me that she herself wasn't surprised at what I just said. In fact, she was in sound agreement with it. The plan I laid out for her was that neither one of us would tell our parents anything about us leaving until the day before we were actually going to leave. For the days that followed, we would spend hours on the phone – planning.

Finally, Sunday arrived. And that next day, we were to leave.

I walked into the kitchen to see mom and dad sitting at the table in their robes, drinking coffee. They were talking and laughing.

They seemed so happy.

Here goes everything.

"Mom, dad, can I talk to you for a moment?"

"Well, good morning to you too, honey," mom heartily responded.

"It's pretty important," I seriously replied.

"Well, come on and have a seat," dad announced.

I went and took my seat.

"What's on your mind?" dad asked.

"This is the hardest thing I've ever had to say to you, and I don't know if I can say it."

Dad then put on his serious face and set his cup down. "What's wrong, son? Don't tell me. You decided not to use the condoms, and now Anna is pregnant?"

Then mom and dad both erupted in laughter.

I couldn't believe it.

Here they were making jokes. I couldn't take it anymore.

"Anna and I are leaving for Berkeley, CA. tomorrow," I blurted out.

Dad then, looking even more serious than before, paused for a few seconds before he announced, "Don't forget to take the condoms with you."

He and mom both again burst out laughing.

They didn't believe me, nor did they think I was serious.

This really angered me.

"Dammit! What is so funny?!" I exclaimed, slamming my fist onto the table.

Then dad looked at me, perplexed, and mom set her cup down. I could tell there would be no more jokes.

"Sweetie, you're serious, aren't you?" mom chimed.

"Yes."

"What has brought all of this about, and why are you just now telling us this?"

"You know, so much has happened lately. And it all started, dad, when you convinced me to put life on hold for Cousin Joey. I should've listened to my better judgement and left with Anna when I had the chance."

"What do you mean?" dad confusingly inquired.

"Oh, come on, dad. You know exactly what I mean. From day one, since he got here; the way he looked at Anna, things he would say, and down to them kissing."

"They did what?" mom surprisingly asked.

"That's exactly right. They even kissed," I retorted. "Dad knows everything about it."

72

Mom looked shocked and annoyed at the same time. "Dennis, why didn't you tell me any of this?"

"Because I didn't want you to get worried and all worked up about it."

"Well, how did you handle it?"

"I gave him the best advice I could give, and that was for him to go and talk to her and straighten things out. But I didn't imagine that they would make plans to run off to another city together."

"You really need to re-think this whole thing through more thoroughly. Have you thought about where you'll live and how you'll live? Where you'll work? How you'll eat and pay bills? How you'll pay for college?" mom retorted.

"Well, first and foremost, we've decided we're not going to college."

"But there's so much more than to living in a city with no family and friends and with pretty much nothing."

"There's where you're wrong, mom. Anna and I have the strongest support, and with it we're bound to have everything we need to survive with and more."

"What's that?"

"Love. You and dad always taught me that with love, anything is possible. Anna and I have love, so I know we can make it."

"But sweetie, you have to be practical…"

"No, no, Patricia. He's old enough to make decisions for himself. How else is he going to learn what life is if he doesn't experience it? His mind is made up. The best we can do now is to respect his decision and be there for him any way we can."

"You're right, Dennis. Then she looked at me and replied, "You have our blessing. When are you leaving?"

"Tomorrow morning."

Chapter 17

"Tomorrow morning?" mom surprisingly announced. "Well, you certainly didn't give us much time to prepare for this. How long have you and Anna been planning this?"

"For a week now. I know this is a short notice, but please trust me on this."

Mom then looked at dad with a worried look on her face, longing for him to say something to change my mind.

"Dennis, we can't just let him up and run off to another city with no money or anything at all."

"Well, what else can we do? He's got his mind made up. He needs to experience it for himself. He's not a little boy anymore."

"I guess you're right." Mom then directing her attention to me replied, "Just know that if you ever need anything, I mean anything at all, or if you ever want to come home, your father and I are here for you."

"I know and thanks, mom."

Then the tears began to well up in mom's eyes as she replied, "My baby's become a man."

Seeing her like this made me want to cry as well.

But I didn't.

Real men don't cry.

There we sat in silence for a minute. Dad, looking at the table with a perplexed look on his face, and mom just crying with an occasional glance at me.

The longer I sat there, the more I felt it pained mom because she knew I was leaving and there was nothing she could do about it.

I finally found the strength to leave. Leave behind the people I called mom and dad, and start a new life.

"Mom, dad," I said, standing up, "don't worry, everything will be just fine. We'll get jobs and find somewhere nice to live, and we'll have everything we need. You'll see."

Dad then looked at me and with the oddest expression replied, "I know, son. Good luck."

On that note, I turned and walked out of the kitchen. I felt it best if I didn't look back.

I went to my room and laid on my bed just staring at the ceiling. A thousand thoughts were racing through my mind at one time.

Then the big question hit me.

Was I being practical?

The whole notion of living off of love sounded nice, but will it pay the bills and put food on the table?

Then reality set in.

We've come this far and there's no turning back.

I reached over on my dresser and picked up my phone and dialed Anna's number.

"Hello."

"Hey babe."

"Oh, hey Will. Listen, I'm actually glad you called. I've been doing some thinking. I've had second thoughts about this whole thing. Don't you think we're moving kind-of fast?"

"Yeah, I was thinking the same thing – at first. But then I realized this is our destiny. With love, we can overcome any obstacle. We can make it. Do you trust me?"

"Yeah, I do, but..."

"Then we should at least try. Besides, my mom and dad said that if we do happen to fall on hard times, we can come home. So what's there to lose?"

"Nothing, I guess. Alright, we can try."

"O.K., so I'll see you in the morning."

"O.K."

"And babe, I love you."

"Alright, I'll see you tomorrow."

"Aren't you gonna tell me you love me too?"

"You know I do. Bye, Will."

"Bye."

Then we hung up.

After the call ended, I just lay there for a moment – thinking.

I noticed she didn't say, "I love you," back to me.

Was it that hard?

"Naw, you're just over-thinking it," I said to myself.

Then I finally shut my eyes and took a nap. I was more tired than I thought.

Chapter 18

I awakened to the smell of eggs and sausage. I yawned and sat up in my bed. Then I began to stretch, and as I did, I heard laughter in the kitchen. The sunlight beamed through my window as I thought of the wonderful night I had last night. I don't remember exactly what I dreamed, only that it was pleasant.

I hadn't slept that good in a long time.

After sitting up in bed for a little bit, reflecting on this peaceful moment I was indulging in, I finally got up and went to the bathroom.

After I was done, I stood and looked in the mirror for a second and then smiled to myself. Then I washed my hands for breakfast.

As I approached the kitchen, I could hear mom and dad talking and laughing.

Then I was there.

Mom was at the stove scrambling the eggs in the skillet while dad was setting the table.

Dad noticed me come in and announced, "Hey, son."

"Hey, dad. Hey, mom."

"Good morning, honey," mom replied as she brought the skillet to the table and began dishing up the plates. Dad helped her prepare the meal, and in no time at all, everything was set.

I surveyed my plate for a minute and saw toast, eggs, sausage, grits, and orange juice to wash it down.

Then my stomach let out a loud grumble. I didn't waste any time sitting down and getting ready to indulge. So much so, I almost forgot my mannerisms. I picked up the fork and this is when I heard dad clear his throat. I looked over at him to see him looking at me. He had his hands folded.

Then he announced, "Will, would you do the honors and lead us into prayer?"

I then put my fork down, folded my hands, and bowed my head.

Then I began: "Heavenly Father, we ask today that You bless this meal we are about to indulge in. We also know that there are many who do not have meals so good as this to eat. There are many without food or homes. Please give them good food to eat and homes for shelter. Bless them as You have blessed us. And also, I pray that You watch over me and Anna and give us all that we need to make it. Cover us in Your loving grace and make sure that we are never without. Guide us and help us to make good decisions under your watchful eye. These things we pray for in the name of Jesus. Amen."

Then I opened my eyes. But before I began to eat, I sat there for a second before I retorted, "So, mom, dad, are you gonna tell me what's really going on? Why the sudden change of heart?"

"What do you mean, Will?" dad asked.

"I mean, why did you take the trouble to cook such a meal when just yesterday, you were totally at odds with me? And you're just laughing and joking like nothing happened yesterday."

"Honey, we're still your parents and will always love you for whatever decision you make. Your father and I talked about it last night, and we decided to give you our full support."

"Thanks, mom."

"Now eat up, your food is getting cold."

81

After we ate, I went and took a nice hot shower and then got dressed. My luggage was already packed, so we got those and went out to the car with very little to say.

Then we got in and headed for Anna's house.

While we drove, dad turned on the radio. That was our excuse for not talking, was we were listening to the radio.

In no time at all, we were there.

I got out and walked to her doorstep, took a deep sigh, and then rang the doorbell.

The door opened, and there was my beloved.

Something about her appearance threw me off. I started to ask her if she got enough sleep last night.

Instead, I asked, "Are you ready?"

"As ready as I'll ever be."

"Aren't your parents coming to see you off?" I inquired.

"They were very unhappy with the decision I've made, so they'll just be staying here."

With that, I helped Anna carry her luggage to the car, and then we were off to the airport.

Once again, silence dominated our journey to our destination.

When we got there, we unloaded our luggage and found our terminal. Our plane was to board soon, and as opposed to having mom and dad wait there with us, I preferred that they didn't. Not because I didn't want them to, but because even though she didn't say anything, I could see and feel the pain this caused mom.

I felt the sooner Anna and I were gone, the better.

"Mr. and Mrs. Warner, I'm going to miss you so much. We'll call and write to you whenever we get a chance," Anna replied.

Then she gave dad a hug and then turned to hug mom.

"We're going to miss you, too," dad responded.

Then it was my turn.

Dad then reached in to hug me and said, "Take care of yourself. And if you need anything, don't hesitate to call."

"I love you, dad," I said, hugging him.

Then I turned to mom, and before I could say anything, she started crying.

"Oh, mom, please don't cry," I said with my eyes starting to water.

Then we heard someone over the intercom announce, "The plane to Berkeley, CA., is now boarding."

"Bye, son," dad said in a half-whisper and then put his arm around mom and led her out.

Then Anna and I went to board our plane.

As we boarded, I got this empty, nauseous feeling in my stomach. Although I knew it wasn't from hunger. It was from the realization of the fact that as much as I hated to admit it, mom was right. Once we got there, what would we do? Where would we live and find jobs? I so badly wanted to turn and run off the plane to mom and dad, and we just go home and forget this nonsense.

But there was no turning back.

Before long, we were seated and ready to leave this city.

When we had our seatbelts on and were ready for take-off, Anna replied, "Will, I'm sorry for everything that happened between me and Joey."

Then she kissed me on the lips.

"It's O.K."

Then we were in the air.

She had her earbuds in her ears, and I had mine in too.

So we didn't talk.

In no time at all, we were landing. There was some turbulence about mid-way through the flight, but everything was O.K.

So far, so good.

When we got off the plane, we caught a cab and decided to stop off at McDonald's. As soon as we got out and walked up to the door, lo and behold, there was a sign on the window that said, "Now hiring for shift managers."

God is good!

We eagerly went in to inquire about the position. Our hunger was the last thing on our minds at this time.

We walked up to the counter and asked the lady there if we could speak to the manager.

"Yeah sure," she replied, chewing her gum.

"Gerald," she called out.

Then a heavy-set, bald man with glasses came from the back area. His appearance was so sloppy, I giggled under my breath to myself. I sensed Anna felt the same humor.

"What can I do for you?" he replied, addressing us.

Anna started to say something, but then I cut her off.

"We were wanting to apply for your shift manager positions," I eagerly responded.

He then looked me over for a second and then replied, "Right this way," leading us to the back area.

We got to his office and saw a desk with papers on it and three chairs. Also, there was a Big Mac that was three-fourths of the way eaten sitting on the desk.

Then I really had to hold back from laughing.

"Have a seat," he announced, and he sat down too.

"So what kind of experience do you have?" he asked.

Anna started to say something, but once again, I cut her off.

"We both were managers at Hardee's back home," I lied.

From there, the interview was smooth sailing. We talked for about forty-five minutes when he finally announced, "You're hired. Be here Monday at 9:00 a.m."

Anna and I both stood up, both shook his hand, and then left. We didn't even stay for the reason we came there in the first place

– to eat.

We were too excited.

We then called a cab and checked into the nearest hotel.

When we got there and got our luggage in and got situated, I told Anna I was going to go and pick up something for dinner.

"Alright, hurry back," she replied, then kissed me.

Then I was gone.

I didn't have to travel, but a few blocks before I ran into a "Gates" barbeque restaurant. I went in and ordered for me and Anna, and then was on my way back to the hotel with the food. I walked in and I heard the shower in the bathroom running.

"Anna, I'm back," I announced.

Suddenly, I thought all hell froze over.

Joey came out of the bathroom with a towel covering his mid-section.

"Joey?!" I retorted.

Then Anna came out of the bathroom wearing nothing but a towel as well.

She looked at me and said, "Hi Will."

I then hopped up in a cold sweat. I started to cry when I started to actually comprehend that it was all a dream.

I got up and walked to the living room to see mom and dad sitting on the couch. They were waiting on me to wake up.

Dad then piped up, "We decided to let you sleep a little extra before you left."

"Mom, dad, let me tell you about this crazy, crazy dream I had."

Chapter 19

I had forgiven Anna for what took place between her and Joey. Although it was hard, believe it or not, to forgive her for the dream I had.

When Anna and I did finally leave, we had a very easy departure and arrival, and it was actually pretty cool – nothing like the dream I had. Both Anna's parents and my parents gave us a nice amount of money to last for quite some time.

But we had to be very frugal with it and spend it sparingly and wisely on necessities only.

When we got there, the only reality that was similar to the dream was that we found jobs very quickly.

Anna was the manager at a bakery store, and I took up work in a warehouse. The salary Anna was making was decent, but what I was getting from the warehouse was amazing.

It was enough for us to live on.

Soon enough, we found a nice apartment. The way we

decorated it was real nice, and life was never better. We wrote to our parents on occasion, as promised, and spent many hours on the phone with them. And on holidays and birthdays, we visited and always had a good time.

We had been on our own for two years now.

On this Easter Sunday, Anna and I are at home with family when dad suddenly announced that he wanted me to come with him to the store to pick up a few more things for tonight's dinner.

I knew he really didn't need me to come, but just wanted to talk.

As we walked to the car, I noticed the air was somewhat humid for this time of the year. Then we were there.

When we got in, dad pulled a pack of cigarettes out of his pocket and offered me one.

"Sure," I replied.

Then he got his out and stuck it in his mouth and lit it up. Afterwards, he lit mine up.

Then we were on our way.

For the first minute or so while he drove, there was silence. There was nothing between us but the smoke from our cigarettes. Then when we stopped at the first red light, he finally piped up, "You know, Will, your mother and I have to admit, we had our doubts at first, but you really came through. We're real proud of you. You and Anna seem real happy together. Are you happy?"

"Yeah, we're very happy."

"You know the key to true happiness in any relationship is love. You do love Anna, don't you?"

"Yeah, and she loves me." I think I already knew where this conversation was going.

"How serious are you and Anna?"

"We're very serious. And I know what you're getting at. Yes, I've thought about marriage, but something happens whenever I get ready to bring it up to Anna. I start to say it, but then nothing comes out of my mouth."

"Well, try a little harder because your mother and I want grandchildren."

Then we were at the store.

As we shopped, I tried to think of something else to talk about.

But to no avail. Dad had already spoken his mind, so there was nothing else to talk about. We got the last of our groceries and went home.

When we got there, mom was at the door waiting for us.

"Did you two have a nice conversation?" she said to dad.

"Yes, we did."

"That's nice, dear. And Anna and I have been talking while you two were gone."

I could imagine about what.

When the dinner was cooked, Anna's parents were there with us as we blessed the meal and ate heartily.

Then we all sat outside and laughed and talked for a while. Suddenly, mom and dad stood up to go in, and then Anna's parents followed. When Anna stood up to go in too, her dad remarked, "No, no, you two stay out here as long as you like and just talk."

Then he turned and went in.

There we sat for a little bit before Anna finally announced, "It's a nice night tonight."

I knew what she wanted to hear. I knew what she wanted to

hear for a long time now – the same thing both our parents wanted to hear, too.

I couldn't take it anymore.

"Anna, there's something I want to ask you."

"Yes, Will?" she attentively asked.

"Do you want to go back home tomorrow?"

That's not what I was supposed to say! But I got cold feet again.

"Sure, whatever you want," she meekly replied, knowing that that's not what I was going to say.

Without another word, I got up and went in the house.

The next day, we headed back home. We said our goodbyes and were on our way.

When we got there, she seemed somewhat upset with me for not asking the question I was going to ask, and she hardly talked to me.

"Listen," I finally replied, "we've got a big day tomorrow, so let's walk up the street to Captain D's and grab a bite to eat and come home and get ready for tomorrow."

"But we have food here."

"I'd really prefer Captain D's."

"Alright, if you say so."

We walked to Captain D's. The whole time we walked, I had this song in my heart that I was listening to.

When we got there, she opened the door and walked in. When she did, I grabbed her arm and swung her around and passionately kissed her on the lips. I then got down on one knee and took her by the hand and responded, "Anna, will you do me the honors and make me the happiest man on the planet and be my wife?"

Then the tears welled up in her eyes.

"Oh, Will, I thought you'd never ask."

"So is that a yes?"

"Yes, I will marry you."

Chapter 20

Preparing for the wedding was the easy part. But I didn't know if I were really ready for the real challenge – life after marriage. We sent many invitations out for this festive event. Of course, our parents were coming, but we also invited some of our co-workers whom we had befriended. Anna and I figured the more to come, the merrier, because we wanted the whole world to know we were in love.

Finally, the big day was here.

Anna got Jan, Michelle, and Sonya to come. On my end, I got Mark and Ritchie from the warehouse.

There Anna was, an angel in all white standing in front of the mirror getting ready to take the biggest step of her life. Her mom was there with her helping her put on the finishing touches and with words of encouragement and support.

"Babe, I'm so proud of you. You look beautiful," Anna's mom said with tears in her eyes. "Will is a good man. I know you'll make him happy."

"I'm real sorry about what happened with Joey, and I won't let anything come between us again."

Whereas at first, Anna's mom was smiling. But then that smile faded. There was something about the way Anna said what she just said. There Anna's mom stood looking at Anna through the reflection of the mirror.

"You do love Will, don't you?"

"Yes, of course."

"Then that's all that matters."

Anna's dad then peeked his head around the corner.

"Are you ready? Everything's in place and we're ready to start."

"As ready as ever," Anna joyfully replied.

Then it was time to get married.

Everyone was seated when the music started. As I stood at the altar, my mind was racing with a thousand thoughts. But then there she was, slowly making her way towards me. When I saw her, she was so beautiful, and all of those thoughts narrowed down to one – making her happy for the rest of our lives.

Then she was there.

As the ceremony went on, and the vows were finally said, there I stood staring in her eyes – searching.

For a moment, I got lost in her eyes. So much so, I didn't even realize I was being spoken to until the pastor cleared his throat to bring me back.

"The ring, please," he repeated.

I then placed it on her finger, and she placed my ring on me.

Then it was time to kiss.

The kiss we shared was the exact same kiss as the very first kiss we shared when we were younger. The same love and passion in that first kiss was also in this kiss.

And so here we were. Our lives were just beginning, and we had a lot of it to go through in getting ready to face the challenges ahead.

I had never been happier, and I know Anna felt the same.

When it was all done and said, I wanted to spend my first night of marriage with my wife alone. Which meant Anna and me leaving with as minimal conversation as possible. As Anna and I tried to make our way out, dad came up to me and asked to speak to me.

"We won't be long, Anna," dad replied, and then we began walking.

"Well, you finally did it. I can't tell you how proud of you your mother and I are. How does this make you feel? You're all grown up."

"I feel like a real man now with real responsibilities."

"I'm glad to hear you say that."

"Be good to her and she will be good to you. And always remember that your mother and I are always here for you."

"Thanks, dad."

We then embraced in a hug.

"I love you, dad," I said, still hugging him.

"I love you, too, son. I know you and Anna probably want to get out of here so you can have some alone time. I won't hold you up anymore."

"Thanks, dad, for everything."

Then dad turned and walked away.

"Now, where did Anna slip off to?" I said under my breath.

I looked to my right and saw Ritchie, my friend from the

warehouse, approaching me.

"Hey, Ritchie, have you seen Anna?"

"Yeah, I was just talking to her."

"She's great, isn't she?"

"The important thing is that you're happy, Will."

He said this with the oddest expression.

Chapter 21

We didn't waste any time planning for our honeymoon. Whereas I was sure Anna would've agreed with me on Bermuda, she really had her heart set on Barbados.

So Barbados it was.

We booked a flight and made a reservation to stay for two weeks.

Before leaving, we said our good-byes and were on our way.

On our way to the airport, I was never more excited. Excited because this alone time with Anna for the next two weeks was greatly needed and much anticipated. But soon this excited feeling was diminished by a terrible queezy feeling I got in my stomach. I thought maybe I was just getting nervous.

This feeling subsided once we boarded the plane.

Once we were seated and secured and about to take off, Anna turned to me and kissed me and replied, "I love you, Will."

Then we were in the air.

I was looking out the window when I thought to ask Anna if she locked the door behind her when we left home. I turned to her to ask her this, only to see her asleep.

"I love you too, babe," I whispered and decided to let her sleep.

Soon, my eyelids grew somewhat heavy, so I decided to shut them.

When I did, I drifted. I drifted off to when I first met Anna that day in school.

Fast-forwarded to the times we spent together growing up and how close we become. Then there was graduation. And then even the dreaded time that Joey spent with us. Finally down to me proposing to her. But then there was a new part. There was an elderly couple sitting on a bench in a park holding hands just watching the children playing. The man then turned and said something to the woman. They looked so much in love.

Was this me and Anna after years of happiness?

Then I woke up.

The dream I had was like watching a sped-up movie version of me and Anna's life together.

I looked over at Anna, who was still sleeping.

Suddenly, that same queezy feeling I got on the way to the airport came back. Once again, I dismissed it as nervousness, but it was very uncomfortable.

Words couldn't describe the relief I felt when we were landing.

When we finally touched down and were landing is when Anna woke up. As the plane slowed to a stop, I took her hand and replied, "Babe, we're finally here."

"Wonderful," she joyfully said. "I can't wait to take in the sights."

I could tell how enthused she was to be here. And I was equally excited. However, I didn't know what kept causing the bad feeling in my stomach.

Maybe I was overly excited.

We both stood up and stretched for a few seconds from our tiring journey, then got off the plane, got our luggage, and found a cab.

We thought finding a cab in a city this busy would be a problem.

Surprisingly, it wasn't. We found one with no problem and was on our way to our hotel.

We checked in at The Luxury Inn Hotel and got to our room. When we got there, we decided to just get some rest for tonight and do a little sight-seeing tomorrow.

We put on our night clothes and, with a sweet kiss, we went to bed.

We both slept peacefully and soundly. My rest lasted only a few hours before I began to toss and turn.

My stomach was in pain again.

I tried to ignore it and go back to sleep, but to no avail.

"Dammit," I whispered to myself as I sat up.

Now I knew for certain I couldn't pass this off as just a little nervousness. I sat there in bed for a few minutes, hoping it would stop.

But it didn't.

This is when I decided to go to the bathroom. I went and had a bowel movement for way longer than I usually did.

When I was done, I came out and looked at the clock. It said 2:13 a.m. I had to get some rest. I got in bed and fell fast asleep.

Before long, I was dreaming of the time when I was younger and I was at home with mom in the kitchen. Dad was at work, and I was helping her make brownies. We had just taken them out of the oven and set them to cool when the doorbell rang. She then told me before going to answer the door, "Don't" eat any. These are for dessert tonight after dinner. Then she went to the living room to see who was at the door. Just as soon as she stepped away, I grabbed one and began to indulge. Lucky for me, I didn't burn my mouth as fast as I was chugging.

Finally, she came back into the kitchen and looked at the plate of brownies.

"William, did you eat a brownie after I told you not to?"

"No ma'am," I lied.

And then she didn't say anything else about it.

It took me years later to realize that she knew I ate a brownie without her wishes.

"Mom, I'm sorry," I mumbled as I was being awakened from my sleep by Anna nudging my arm.

"Will, wake up," she kept saying.

Finally, I was awake.

I looked at her and saw that she was dressed and ready to get her day started.

"I know the first place I want to go today," she eagerly replied.

"Babe, do you mind if I get more rest. I was up half the night in the bathroom."

The icy cold look she gave me after that response could've put a hole in someone's heart.

"Sure, I don't mind," she replied.

Chapter 22

After resting for a few more hours, I finally awakened. My eyes were open, but I just lay there. It was so peaceful. Then I decided to get up because I did promise Anna we'd get to tour the city today.

Wouldn't want to make the wife mad.

We started our day with, "Good morning," and a sweet kiss. Then I headed to the bathroom and had a nice, long, hot shower. The water was very soothing and washed away the troubles of last night. I finally came out and got dressed. It was then we decided on I-hop for breakfast.

While we were on our way to I-hop, whereas at first I was extremely hungry, after a little while, I didn't even notice the hunger because I was busy taking in the sights on the way there.

In no time at all, we were there.

We walked in and as soon as we did, a young, brown-haired gentleman addressed us and then led us to a table. I was enjoying the aroma of freshly cooked pancakes when I suddenly heard Anna reply to the waiter, "Do you have anything else, preferably by a window?"

"Of course," he said and led us to a different table.

We sat down and he said, "I'll be back with your menus."

Then he was gone.

As soon as he left, Anna replied, "Isn't this wonderful?"

"Yeah, it is."

My hand was on the table when Anna placed her hand on top of mine and said, "I was thinking that maybe later on tonight, we can..."

Before she could finish, the waiter was back with our menus.

"My name is Steven, and I will be your server today. What can I get you for drinks?" he announced, placing our menus in front of us.

"I'll have Pepsi," I piped up.

"And Pepsi for me too," Anna responded.

"I'll have that out shortly," he said and then left again.

"Now, where were we?" I longingly said to Anna, looking at

her across the table.

"I was just wondering if you wanted to play that game tonight, we haven't played in a while."

"Sounds nice," I said, envisioning it in my mind.

I looked in her eyes, but I didn't know what I was looking for – maybe a reason. I started to ask her for a reason as to why – why all of this all of a sudden?

Then Steven returned with our drinks. He set them down in front of us and replied, "Are you ready to order yet?"

Still looking at Anna, I responded, "I'll have the Belgian waffles with scrambled eggs and sausage."

Anna then broke her gaze from me and directed her attention to Steven and announced, "I'll have the pancakes with eggs over easy and bacon."

Neither one of us had looked at our menu before deciding.

"I'll have that out shortly," he said, picking up our menus, and then he was gone again.

The tension was so heavy, you could cut the air between us with a knife.

Finally, Anna said, "What do you say we go back to the hotel?"

"But what about breakfast?"

"What about it?"

"Alright, let's go."

And then we got up and left I-hop and headed back to the hotel.

When we got to our room, Anna opened the door and stepped in. I then swung her around and passionately kissed her. She kissed me back, and while we kissed, we made our way to the bed.

Then there we were in bed. I stopped kissing her for a moment to look into her eyes. Next, we both got undressed and were naked.

"Will, I really do love you."

"I know."

Then we made love.

The rest of the trip could've been considered the best time of our lives.

We did a lot of sight-seeing and eating at good restaurants. Aside from that, every other time we were making love.

Before we knew it, the trip was over, and time to return home.

On the plane on the way back, I asked her, "Did you enjoy it?"

"I had the time of my life," she responded and placed her head on my shoulder.

Soon enough, we were landing.

When we got home, we both had the same thing in mind – more lovemaking.

But suddenly that idea was halted. As soon as we were kissing, I hopped up and ran to the bathroom.

My stomach was hurting again.

I stayed in there for over an hour before I came out.

"Babe, I think we need to make me a doctor's appointment."

"I'll call him first thing in the morning."

Chapter 23

"The doctor will see you now, William," a very pretty nurse came out to the waiting room and announced.

As Anna and I stood up and began to walk to the back area, I tried to avoid looking at this pretty nurse too much for fear of Anna sensing my physical lust.

Then it was time to meet Dr. Wheeler.

We were led to a room by the pretty nurse. Anna and I both sat down and then she informed us, "The doctor will be with you shortly."

I was looking at Anna when I responded with, "Thank you," to the nurse.

Then I looked at her, and she was just looking at me for a few seconds before she turned to leave.

When she closed the door behind her, I directed my attention back to Anna and replied, "I hope it's nothing serious – maybe just a stomach flu."

"Yeah, hopefully."

Something in Anna's tone when she said this didn't sound quite right.

Maybe she had picked up on the flirtatious vibe between me and the pretty nurse.

After about a moment of silence, the doctor walked in.

He was a rather tall man with a neatly shaved mustache maybe in his early fifties.

"Hi," he announced, extending his hand to shake mine. "I'm Casey Wheeler."

I shook his hand, and then he shook Anna's hand.

"What brings you here today?" he asked.

"Well, I've been having some pain in my stomach. It's very uncomfortable and I find myself in the bathroom a lot."

"Let's start with your vitals."

He then walked to the desk, opened it, and pulled out a stethoscope. He checked me out and responded, "Everything's normal there."

He then took my blood pressure and examined me.

Once he was done, he asked, "How often do you get these pains in your stomach?"

"Maybe four or five times a day."

"When was the last time you saw a doctor or had a check-up?"

"It's been years now."

"I'd like to get an X-ray and also a stool sample. I should have the results back in a few days. In the meantime, I'm prescribing Nexium for you."

"Sounds good."

The next few days for Anna and me were strenuous. We were both on pins and needles contemplating the results of the doctor's visit. We tried to be up-beat and positive, but the idea of the possibility of something bad lingered between us. However, what was really amazing was that it had been two days since the doctor's visit, and my stomach hadn't given me any problems.

I actually felt in good spirits.

So much so that I decided that me and Anna should go out to dinner and a movie. Anna got dressed up real nice, and I looked pretty decent as well. I put on my best cologne, and we headed to an all-you-can-eat buffet.

After dinner, we were just in time to catch the new scary movie.

We had quite a good time that night.

When we got home, we sat down in the kitchen and we both had a glass of wine. We talked about our lives and memories we had together in our childhood. We laughed, reminisced and drank.

Finally, we went to bed and made love.

I didn't have to go to the bathroom once.

I awoke to the sunlight shining through the window. Both Anna and I were naked. Her arm was draped over my chest.

What a night last night!

I then gently kissed her on her forehead.

"Babe, wake up."

She slowly opened her eyes and smiled and whispered, "Good morning, handsome."

Then the phone rang.

I reached over on the nightstand and answered it.

"Hello."

"Hi, is this William?"

"Yes."

"This is Dr. Wheeler. I have the results back from the lab."

"Well, is it a stomach virus or what?"

"It's not a stomach virus. Please come in and see me."

Chapter 24

"Will, come on now. You've tried for the last fifteen minutes deciding on what to wear. If I didn't know any better, I'd swear that you were trying to purposely be late to this appointment."

The truth was I was actually trying to be late to the appointment because when Dr. Wheeler said, come in and see him, it sounded urgent.

I feared the worst.

"I'm just looking for my blue-striped shirt," I lied.

"I found it," I finally announced, so as not to let on to Anna what my intent was.

But it was so obvious.

When I couldn't find anymore reasons to stall, I replied, "O.K., are we ready?"

"After you," Anna sarcastically said, gesturing with her hand.

Then we were out the door.

When we got there and entered the hospital, I paused for a second and took a deep breath. Then we went to check-in.

While we sat and waited, I really hoped that the same pretty nurse who was here last time was here today. After a few minutes of waiting, sure enough, the pretty nurse came out into the waiting room and announced, "William, the doctor will see you now."

Seeing her gave me some relief. But I was careful not to let it show to Anna.

As we followed the nurse to the back area, it took me a second or two to realize it, but Anna and I were holding hands.

Finally, we reached the room.

"He will be with you shortly," she announced and smiled at me and then turned and walked out and closed the door behind her.

I became so nervous awaiting the arrival of Dr. Wheeler and hearing what he had to say. My palms began to sweat, and my heart began to race.

"Look, Anna," I began, "I want you to know that whatever happens in this visit, I..."

"Oh look, Will," Anna happily replied, cutting me off, "look at this candy ring on the floor."

I looked at it and then she went to pick it up. She then brought it back and sat down. And sure enough, it had to be orange.

"It's the same color candy ring I gave you in eighth grade," I said, studying it.

"Yeah, it sure is. Imagine that," she replied.

"Do you remember how jealous Abel Johnson got when he saw me give you that ring because he had a crush on you?"

"I remember," she said, laughing.

In no time at all, we were down memory lane just laughing and talking about the different events that took place in our lives.

But then came a point when we were laughing, we both stopped laughing. Suddenly as if in a trance, we both fell into a gaze just staring into each other's eyes. A point came when, as I was looking into her eyes, I saw the same little girl who approached me when we first met, and she asked me if she could color in the coloring book with me.

Then our gaze was broken.

The door opened, and in stepped Dr. Wheeler.

"William, thank you for coming," he announced.

"Well, is it just a stomach flu or a virus?"

Suddenly, he looked very sad as he replied, "I'm sorry, William. You have stage four abdominal cancer and an expected time of five months to live."

"What?!" Anna screamed out.

Suddenly I couldn't hear anything that was being said. It was like I was in my own world. I could see things, but I couldn't.

"How long did you say I have to live?" I finally piped up.

"About five months; give or take a few weeks."

Chapter 25

My whole world was shattered. I didn't even want to live anymore. But I didn't have to worry about that because in about five months, that whole notion would become a reality.

It's been three days since I heard the terrible news, and I still haven't told mom and dad. I wanted to prolong it for as long as possible. However long that may be.

Anna's in the bedroom crying, which has been pretty much what she's been doing since she heard the news. I'm sitting on the couch in the living room staring at the phone while contemplating whether I should call mom and dad.

Finally, I picked up the phone as a tear rolled down my cheek. As I dialed the number, I tried to find a way to compose myself so as to soften the blow for them.

Then it rang.

"Hello."

"Oh my God, dad! It's terrible."

"William, what's wrong? What's going on?"

"Dad, it's terrible."

"William, listen to me. Calm down. Take a few breaths and tell me what's going on."

"Dad, I have abdominal cancer and only about five months to live."

"What?!"

Then I could hear mom in the background say, "What's going on?"

Dad then responded, "It's William. I think he should tell you himself."

Then I heard mom on the phone, "William, what's going on? Are you alright?"

"No mom, I'm not. I have stage four abdominal cancer and about five months to live."

Then I heard the phone drop.

"Patricia," dad screamed.

"What's going on?" I yelled.

"She just passed out," dad said into the phone.

"Is she going to be O.K.?"

"Yeah, she'll be fine. William, pack your things up and come home."

"Alright, dad. I'll get packed up tonight."

I slowly hung the phone up. When I finally did hang up, right then and there, I had the biggest cry of my life. Then I felt a hand on my shoulder followed by Anna's soothing voice.

"Will, it's going to be O.K. You'll get through this alright. You'll see."

But then I noticed something very strange, and it made me freeze.

"Anna, what do you mean I'll get through this alright instead of we'll get through this alright?"

"Oh, it was no mistake. You heard me right. I'm not going to be here with you. I'm leaving you for another man."

Chapter 26

"What did you say?" I winced, thinking I heard her wrong.

"That's right, Will. I'm leaving you for someone else. His name is Jeff."

"But how? Why?"

I met him three months ago when I went to work. Then, some days when I would go to work, I would visit with him. We were having an affair."

"You bitch!"

"I'm sorry, Will. I really am. I just can't be with someone who's dying and is so needy."

She then walked into the bedroom and a few seconds later came out with two suitcases she had already packed up. Then she proceeded to the front door. She opened the door and then stopped and turned to look at me.

"Take care of yourself, Will."

With that, she was gone.

As soon as the door closed, I screamed out, "No! God, what have I done for this?"

I then pinched my left elbow to see if I could awaken from this nightmare. But the sting from the pinch let me know that I was not dreaming and that this was all too real.

Now I really wanted to end my life. I just lost my wife, and I will be dead in about five months.

All of this happening to me now led me to believe that suicide would be the perfect escape route.

I had nothing left to live for, and I didn't want to live anymore. Each second I stayed alive, I became more disgusted with life, and I wanted to end it all.

But instead, I got up and went into the bedroom and began packing my things to go home and live out the rest of my days with mom and dad.

After packing most of my stuff, I slumped back on the bed. I looked over at the nightstand, and the clock read 11:32 p.m. I laid my head down. I then took a deep breath through my nostrils and then exhaled through my mouth. I did this again and again. Surprisingly, this actually calmed me. It calmed me to a point of rational thinking and clarity.

I decided to call dad again. I got up and went into the living room. I sat on the couch and picked the phone up. I just sat there for a moment, staring at the phone.

Then I dialed dad.

"Hello."

"Hey, dad. It's me."

"Will, have you already started packing? Do you want your mother and I to come get you?"

"Yes, I've already started packing, and no, I don't need you to come get me."

"Yes, son, please hurry. The sooner you get home, the better. We'll get you to a different doctor and get a second opinion. We're gonna fight this thing."

"Well, looks like I'll be fighting alone."

"What do you mean? You'll have your mom, me, and Anna."

"I'll have you and mom, but not Anna. She left me."

"All the more reason to come home."

Chapter 27

When dad said this, I hung up. There was nothing left to say.

I slowly stood up and made my way to the bedroom. Not to pack, but just to rest.

I was extremely drained.

When I got to the bedroom, I turned off the light and sat on the bed. Before climbing in bed to rest, I started thinking – remembering. I remembered the times with Anna; good and bad. There were a lot of good times, but bad ones too. Suddenly, the bad ones over-shadowed the good ones as they raced to my mind. There I saw them and reflected on them.

From cousin Joey, to the mean things she would say sometimes, to the horrid, evil look she sometimes would throw me, and finally up to her leaving me.

As I sat there and reflected, whereas at first I was tired, that tired feeling soon left. My blood began to boil because I couldn't find any answers as to why she treated me this way when I was nothing but good to her.

Soon, this rage came out as I forgot about being tired. This rage gave me energy as I quickly and fervently began to pack.

Before long, I was done.

Then I could hear dad's words, "The sooner you come home, the better."

I sat down, picked up my phone, and called a cab. I was headed to the airport. When he finally got there, I turned all the lights out and walked out the door.

I didn't look back.

On the plane, I was so absorbed into thoughts of that bitch, I hardly noticed the mild turbulence.

In no time at all, we were landing.

When I got off the plane and to the station, there I saw mom and dad. They both ran to me. Finally, they embraced me in a hug. As mom cried out, "My baby, my baby," the tears streamed down her face.

I never saw her this emotional before.

After a lengthy hug, dad looked at me and said, "Son, how are you feeling?"

"Well, my stomach hurts a little."

"In the morning, I'll have you looked at by a different doctor who'll give you a second opinion."

"Sounds good."

Then we went home.

When we got home, I walked in and anxiously made my way to my bedroom. Then I lay across my bed, and there I began to heavily sob.

Why was all of this happening to me now?

Then I heard mom at the door say, "Will, if you need anything..."

Dad then piped up, "He needs to be alone. Just let him rest."

As I heard the footsteps walk away from my door, I heard a voice in my head say, "Get up and go get your wife."

But how?

Then reality set in.

It's over – forever.

Falling asleep was no problem because I was so tired. But

getting up the next morning – there was the challenge. Until the aroma of fresh cut applewood bacon hit my nostrils.

I slowly sat up to see the sun beaming through my window.

Another day.

But my first without Anna.

God, give me the strength.

Then I got up to go use the bathroom. I washed up and brushed my teeth, then went to join mom and dad for breakfast.

When I got there, I saw both of them sitting at the table in their night clothes, each with a cup of coffee in hand. Then I saw my area of the table with a plate of bacon, eggs, sausage, rice, and a cup of hot coffee to wash it down.

It made my mouth water.

I then joined them at the table.

I sat down and picked up my fork ready to indulge when I heard dad clear his throat.

"Are we forgetting something?" he replied.

"Oh yeah," I quickly responded as I bowed my head and closed my eyes.

"Thank You for this meal. Amen."

"Amen," mom and dad replied.

There was nothing else to say.

About half-way through my meal, dad announced, "I scheduled you for a 1:00 p.m. appointment with Dr. Parks."

"Thanks, dad."

When I was done, I picked up my plate and cup and took them and placed them in the sink. Then as I headed out the kitchen to go back to my room, dad replied, "Will, I'd like to talk to you for a moment."

"Sure, just give me a minute."

Then I disappeared down the hall to my room to get dressed. When I got to my room, I closed the door behind me and then stood there staring at my bed for a moment. I so badly wanted to just dive in my bed and take a very long nap.

But then I forced myself to get dressed. Once I was dressed, I started unpacking my things – a pair of jeans here, a sweater there. Until finally I came across a photograph of me and Anna on our honeymoon.

We looked so happy.

But then I began to tear the photo up, realizing that this false sense of happiness was just an illusion.

As the tears welled up in my eyes, I frivolously wiped them away.

"No, I'm done crying. It's time to move on," I said out loud while opening my door.

There I saw dad. He was dressed now too.

"Dad, you wanted to speak to me?"

"Yeah, let's go sit on the porch."

As we walked through the living room to the porch, my stomach began to hurt again.

Then we went outside.

"Have a seat," he remarked without looking at me. And then he sat down.

"Son, I really wanted to talk to you about Anna."

"Anna? Don't you think I have bigger problems to worry about than Anna?"

"Come with me," he said, standing up.

We walked down the stairs and to the side of the house to the garage. He opened the door, and there it was; my baby.

"It's still in good condition," dad announced.

There I stood staring at the greatest present I ever received in my life. Then a grin came across my face, followed by a few chuckles.

"What's funny?" dad inquired.

"I just remember when you bought me this for my graduation present and how foolishly I didn't want to take it to Berkeley with me and Anna because I wanted to show you and mom that Anna and I could make it and survive with nothing but love alone.

It seemed both dad and I fell into a trance staring at this beauty when he finally announced, "Well, do you wanna take her for a spin?"

"Sure," I excitedly replied.

"Alright, just be back in time for your doctor's appointment."

Chapter 28

I drove to the spot Anna and I went to the first night I got the car. As I sat there over-looking the city, I remembered what Anna said to me right there after we made love.

She looked longingly into my eyes and said, "I will always, always love you."

If that's true, then where are you now?

Is someone loving you better than I could?

As soon as I thought this, my stomach began to hurt again – badly. In fact, I think this was the worst one yet. I doubled over and held myself to fight the pain.

But to no avail.

I started the car up and then drove away.

I had a doctor's appointment to get to.

When I got home, mom and dad were already outside waiting on me. Dad hurried to the car as mom was already getting in.

"We have to hurry, Will," dad replied. "It takes about twenty minutes to get there and it's already 12:45 p.m."

"Don't worry. I'll get us there."

As I drove, I purposely speeded to get to our destination. Neither mom nor dad protested or told me to slow down. They both knew the importance of this appointment.

Finally, we arrived there. I parked and then we rushed in to get me checked in.

Once I was checked in, I was about to sit down when the nurse came from behind the door and announced, "William, the doctor will see you now."

I looked at mom and dad, then took a deep breath, and then began my journey to the back area to meet Dr. Parks.

As we followed the nurse, my stomach once again began to irritate me. But this time, I didn't think it was the cancer. It was from nervousness. I was nervous because a second opinion could mean that the first diagnosis was wrong, and I wouldn't die in five months.

She led us to an empty room and announced, "Dr. Parks will be in shortly."

Then she left.

There we all sat in silence and awaited the arrival of the man who could change my life forever.

About ten minutes later, the knob turned, and I felt a lump in my throat. In stepped Dr. Parks.

The first thing I noticed about him was the gray and black streaks in his neatly combed hair.

"I'm Dr. Parks," he announced, extending his hand to shake dad's.

"I'm Dennis," dad said, shaking his hand. "This is my wife, Patricia, and this is William."

After the hand shaking was done, dad piped up, "We're here for a second evaluation for William. The first doctor told him he had abdominal cancer with an expected time of about five months to live. We were hoping you could tell us something different."

Dr. Parks suddenly looked sad and replied, "Yes, certainly I can run some tests and see what I come up with."

"Can we get started as soon as possible?" mom interjected. "Time is the most precious commodity we have now."

The tests were run as we sat at home waiting for a response as to the results. Finally a few days later, we were eating breakfast when the phone rang. I jumped up to answer it and in doing so, spilled the hot cup of coffee in my hand onto the floor.

My heart beat a mile a minute as I raced to the phone.

"Hello," I frantically said, answering it.

"Yes, this is Dr. Parks."

"Well, what are the results?"

"I'm sorry, William. The results I got are the same as the previous doctor but with a slight variation. Instead of five months to live, you have about ten. Unless of course...,"

"What?"

"William, answer me a question. Do you believe in miracles?"

"Yes, I do."

"That's all I needed to know."

Chapter 29

When he said this, I began to nash my teeth in disgust. I thought he was toying with me. Here was a critical situation, and he was joking. I started to hang up.

"William, there just so happens to be a doctor who specializes in the type of cancer you have and also in the terminal stage. He has an extremely successful track record with the reversal of the progression of the cancer in his patients and making them cancer-free."

I paused for a moment.

There is hope!

I wanted to scream.

"Go on, I'm listening," I replied, masking my excitement.

"His name is George Hansel, and I've already spoken to him about you. He wants you to come into the office and meet with him."

"Perfect. When?"

"He'll be in on Thursday at 11:00 a.m."

"Thank you so much, Dr. Parks. You don't know what this means to me."

"Actually, I really do. You see, I lost my wife two years ago to cancer. Dr. Hansel, at the time, was in Germany, making people cancer-free before coming here to the United States. Had he have gotten here sooner, my wife would have lived."

"I'm sorry to hear that."

"There is hope for you, William. Please be here on Thursday at 11:00 a.m."

"Absolutely."

"I'll be praying for you. Goodbye."

"Bye. And thanks again."

When I hung up the phone, I turned to mom and dad, who were now standing behind me. I embraced them in a hug. As the tears rolled down my face, I told them what Dr. Parks said. We were standing there hugging and crying when mom looked to the ceiling and said, "Thank you, Lord."

Then dad replied, "Son, you've been given a second chance. This journey you're about to take won't be easy. It's going to take a lot of dedication and even more faith. Are you up to it?"

"Yes."

I was actually more up for it than ever.

For the next few days, we spent a lot of time praying, strengthening our hearts and our faith.

Then came Wednesday night, and we were all seated at the table for dinner. Dad said a very powerful and enriching prayer before we ate. His words were emotion-driving and encouraging. When he was done and we all said, "Amen," we began to indulge.

Mom made macaroni and cheese, baked fish, and steamed broccoli with iced tea to wash it down.

Oh, it was good!

Then, when we were done, we set the dishes in the sink and decided to wash them in the morning.

"Good night, mom. Good night, dad," I announced, then headed to my room.

They knew for a fact I wasn't going to sleep just yet. I was going to pray.

When I got to my room, I kneeled at my bed and folded my hands and began, "God, you've always been good to me. I pray now that this opportunity is a second chance for life. Give me the strength I need to do this. Help me stay strong the entire time. And I have faith that through your loving grace, I will come out victorious in the end. And Lord, I forgive Anna for the wrong she has done me. I say a special prayer for her. These things I pray for in the name of Jesus. Amen."

I then stood up, climbed into bed and pulled the covers over my head. In no time at all, I was asleep.

And there I was coloring in my coloring book with Anna when we were children. This was the first day we met. Then I started seeing images of our lives together as we grew up and got closer and closer. The next thing I knew, Anna was sitting next to me on the couch as she announced, "I'm leaving you for another man."

The anger and fury that rose up was like never before.

But then suddenly I heard a soothing voice reply, "Did you really forgive Anna? If you can forgive Anna with your heart, I will answer your prayer."

I then hopped up to see the sun shining through my window. I was sweating profusely.

Then I said to myself in a half-whisper, "He wants me to forgive Anna with my heart."

Right there, sitting up in bed, I closed my eyes and began, "Lord, I forgive Anna with all my heart for what she has done. I know that whatever You do is in Your will and Your planned timing. It is no longer in my hands. I forgive Anna for everything and I trust that You will make Your decision in Your own accordance. Amen."

Then I got out of bed – spirited and refreshed.

Was he already answering my prayer?

Then a knock at my door.

I opened it to see dad standing there with the oddest expression on his face. I could detect a trace of a smile on his mouth.

"Are you ready for breakfast?" he asked.

"Yeah, just let me get dressed."

"Alright."

Then he turned and disappeared down the hall.

I got dressed and in no time at all, I was ready for breakfast.

We had a nice meal in which we said grace before we ate. When we were done, I washed the dishes, including the ones from last night.

Silence loomed throughout the house until it was time to go to my appointment.

The one feeling that filled each of us was the same – anticipation.

We were optimistic that there was hope that I could live.

I was sitting on the couch in the living room when dad announced, "Well, son, it's 10:30 a.m. Are you ready?"

"As ready as I'll get."

Chapter 30

I was ready to open the door to a cancer-free life.

A second chance.

Mom then walked into the living room, ready to go.

"Are you ready?" dad asked her.

"I'm very ready. But first...," she announced, grabbing dad's and my hand. Then she closed her eyes and began.

She said a beautiful prayer of hope and a brighter day around the corner.

Then we were on our way to meet Dr. Hansel.

When we got there, dad parked and we slowly made our way out of the car. I had a thousand thoughts racing through my mind at one time. Even though we parked much closer this time than we did on the last visit, the walk to the entrance seemed to take a lot longer to get there this time.

Finally, we arrived at the door.

As we walked in, a person in a wheelchair was coming out. He looked very sickly and as if he hadn't eaten in a while.

Then we went to check in.

As we sat there and waited, I tried to develop a confident air. Then the nurse came out and said, "William, Dr. Hansel will see you now."

"You got this," I said under my breath and then stood up to go meet Dr. Hansel.

As I walked to the back, I looked behind me to make sure mom and dad were there behind me. Even though they were there, I still felt alone. Alone because I knew that if Dr. Hansel couldn't come through, that's exactly where I'd be – alone, but in death.

We followed the nurse to an empty room. She then very politely replied, "He will be in shortly." Then she left and closed the door behind her.

We sat patiently and waited. Then longer. And longer. Finally, a young man, whom at first glance I thought was too young to be a doctor, stepped in.

"Hi," he heartily announced. "I'm Dr. Hansel."

He then shook each one of our hands. Then he directed his attention to me.

"You must be William," he replied.

"Yes, sir," I nervously responded.

"Sorry, I'm so late. I was going over the results from your lab work."

I listened with intentness.

"I must say it does look pretty bad. That's the bad news. The good news is there's hope. You can be cured. I've treated several patients with cancer in the terminal stage and beat the odds."

"But what does Will have to do on his end to make sure this process works?" dad inquired.

The treatment is a combination of aggressive chemotherapy, surgery to remove as many cancer cells as I can from his abdomen, and a new drug that is still considered in the testing phase to rid out the cancer cells that I might miss in surgery. What's needed from Will is commitment to procedure and to be strong."

Dr. Hansel then fixed his gaze upon me.

"I'm not going to lie to you, Will, it's not going to be easy. In

145

the end, it all comes down to how badly you want to live."

"When can we get started?" I announced.

"The sooner, the better. We only have about ten months."

Chapter 31

And so my treatment began. As Dr. Hansel told me, it wasn't easy. It was very rigorous and tedious.

Then there I was sitting across from Anna, staring directly into her eyes. I had so much I wanted to say to her. But I felt so much pain in my heart, my mouth wouldn't move to let me say anything. Finally, I was able to utter the word, "Why?"

Her mouth then crooked into a grin as she slowly replied, "I think you know exactly why. I never loved you."

I hopped up in a cold sweat. I then winced and grabbed my stomach. It was in terrible pain from the stitches.

Something then told me to tear the stitches out with my hands. Or better yet, go driving and speeding down the highway and hit a pole or go over the embankment.

I had no reason to live. I lost the most important thing in my entire life. She left me for another man.

What more was there to say?

I climbed out of bed still holding my stomach because of the pain. I then quickly flipped on my light switch, grabbed my keys, and headed for the door.

When I got outside, a cool gust of wind hit me. As I made my way to the car, the wind picked up. Finally, I was at my car about to get in and go end my life altogether when I heard a very calm voice that sounded like it was coming from the wind itself say, "You're fighting for a second chance. There is goodness that lies ahead. Just keep your faith strong."

"But why?! Why?!" I shouted. "I just want to end it all now. No one has life harder than me."

"You have to be shown," that mellow voice whispered.

Suddenly, I heard dad's voice call out, "Will, what the hell are you doing out here?"

I looked over to see him approaching me with great strides.

"I've been looking for you. Your cousin Joey's sister just called. He's in the hospital, and it's pretty serious.

"What happened?" I piped up.

"She says he was on a ladder at his house and fell off."

"He's going to be O.K., isn't he?"

"Apparently not. He's paralyzed from the neck down."

I slapped myself in the face to wake up from this nightmare. But the sting from the slap let me know it was all too real.

As dad and I made our way back to the house, I heard that voice whisper again, "You have to be shown."

When I got to my room, I jumped in bed and tried as hard as I could to fall fast asleep.

I felt something nudging my arm as I awakened to see the sun shining through my window. And there was dad standing there, but with tears streaming down his face.

"Your cousin Joey took his own life about an hour ago. And you have an appointment today with Dr. Hansel. So are you doing this or not?"

Then I remembered that voice again, "You have to be shown."

Right there, I knew what I was being shown.

"Yeah dad, I'm ready."

Chapter 32

Joey's death was another hard hit to me. But it was certainly an eye opener. I realized that life is hard. But it's the decisions we make to deal with it that matters.

I fought tooth and nail with mom and dad by my side every step of the way to beat cancer. We spent a lot of time in church praying. When we weren't doing that, we would be at home laughing and talking, trying to mask over the pain that lingered in our hearts.

I thought about Anna often, and every time I did, I said a prayer for her.

Then one day, me, mom, dad, and Dr. Hansel were sitting in his office. He had a folder with a bunch of papers he was looking at.

Finally, he extended his hand to shake mine and very heartily replied, "Congratulations, Will. Your cancer is in remission."

At that point, everything was silent to me. It was like I was in my own world.

Did he say what I think he just said?

Could it be true?

Yes, I beat cancer!

It took me a few seconds to snap out of my trance. When I finally did, I looked over and saw mom hugging dad and bawling and crying like never before, followed up with the occasional, "Thank you, Jesus."

They then embraced me in a hug, and we were all crying.

Dr. Hansel then stood up and replied, "Congratulations again, Will. I'll give you all some time alone now."

With no further words, Dr. Hansel left the room.

"Dad, I did it!" I happily announced.

"Yes, you did, son. God is good all the time."

"Yes, He is," I responded.

Suddenly, a knock at the door.

"Come on in," I joyfully replied.

In stepped the very pretty nurse who was assistant to Dr. Hansel for my treatment. She had a piece of paper in her hand.

"I don't mean to interrupt," she politely said, "but I think you dropped this, William."

Then she handed me the piece of paper. It was the grocery list I made out this morning. It must've fallen out of my pocket.

"Thank you, Sarah," I slowly replied.

Then she stood there looking at me and smiling for a few seconds.

"Is there anything else?" I confusedly asked.

"I don't know. Is there?" she said, still smiling.

"Honey, I think that's our cue," dad said to mom. "Will, we're going to take a walk down the hall."

"Come on, babe," dad said to mom, guiding her out.

Then they were gone.

Here me and Sarah were all alone.

And she was waiting. Waiting on me to say all the right things.

But I was nervous.

I tried to say something, but I began to stutter and ramble.

Finally, in the middle of my rambling, she laughed and announced, "Yes, I will go out with you."

Chapter 33

The date was set for the next day at 5:00 p.m. We decided upon Chelly's Café. Whereas I had never been there before, I heard the food was excellent. Not only that, but also it would be a nice place for a first date and just to sit and talk and get to know each other better.

That night at home, mom and dad acted as if I were new to this and tried to coach me on proper etiquette for the date.

Wear your best cologne.

Be yourself.

Be confident.

Compliment her favorably.

Be a gentleman.

Be ten minutes early.

They drilled me on this so much, I finally interrupted and said, "Mom, dad, I hate to be rude, but I already know all of this.

And besides, I should get some good rest so I can be prepared for the date."

"He's right, babe," dad said to mom. "Let him take it from here."

"Thanks, mom and dad. I love you guys for everything."

With that, I kissed mom on the cheek and gave dad a hug. Just as I was about to walk away, I was still hugging dad when he held me a little longer and replied, "Son, I'm so proud of you."

"Thanks, dad," I responded.

Then I turned and went to my room. When I got there, I closed my door behind me. Then I stood and looked in the mirror for a minute.

"You did it," I said to myself.

I felt like shouting for joy.

But I didn't.

Instead, I climbed in bed, clothes and shoes on, and went to sleep. All of this was happening so fast, to having a terminal diagnosis of cancer to being cancer-free to meeting Sarah.

I needed time to comprehend all of this.

In no time at all, I was sleep. And then in no time at all, my alarm clock was going off and I opened my eyes to see the sun shining through my window.

Thank You, God for giving me another chance.

Even though it didn't feel like I had been asleep very long, I felt very well rested.

I then got up to begin my day.

Feeling so refreshed this day, I did ten push-ups and then ten sit-ups. I then bowed my head and said a prayer of thankfulness to the Lord.

I was ready to begin a new life!

When I was done, I went to the bathroom to shower.

I turned the water on to a little hotter than usual. When I came out, I got dressed and could smell mom's bacon frying in the skillet.

I didn't waste any time making my way to the kitchen.

When I got there, the table was set, and there were my wonderful parents seated and waiting on me.

I took my seat, and we joined hands, and dad said a marvelous grace for the food.

Then we ate.

Never had food tasted so good!

While we ate, we talked and laughed and were so grateful.

There was a lot to be grateful for.

When we were done, I volunteered to do the dishes. While I washed, I thought about Sarah. I was just imagining her beautiful face and her gorgeous smile.

How would our first date be?

Hopefully, one I'll never forget.

When I was done washing dishes, I dried them and put them up. I then decided to go sit on the porch for a while.

I went outside and sat down in the chair dad usually sits in. I looked out across the front yard and began to reminisce. I looked to my left and remembered that was the spot Joey told me to go long and threw a perfect spiral, and I caught it and yelled, "Touchdown!"

I sat there for a while reminiscing when suddenly dad came to the door and announced, "Will, you've been out there for some time now. It's already 1:13 p.m."

My, how time flies!

I got up and went in the house leaving the memories in the front yard.

Chapter 34

As I stood looking in the mirror about to go meet up with Sarah, I thought to myself of how I'd never imagined I'd be with another woman other than Anna. And now here I was about to meet up with this nice young lady for a date.

Then I lifted my arm and smelled it.

Dammit, too much cologne. But it was already on me, so I just went with it.

"Mom," I announced as I came out of my room and into the living room where she and dad were, "do you think I have on too much cologne?"

"No, sweetie," she responded. "I think it's just fine."

"You look good, son," dad replied. "Go on and have a good time."

I looked at the clock and it said 4:28 p.m.

"I better get going," I said and hurried for the door.

When I got outside and got to my car, I realized that I didn't say goodbye. Before opening the car door, I whispered, "Bye mom and dad."

And then I was on my way to meet up with Sarah.

As I drove, I kept looking at my watch. It was 4:45 p.m. and Chelly's Café was only a few blocks away. I'd be there in time to be ten minutes early.

Finally, when I arrived, I pulled in the parking lot and parked. I sat there for a few seconds and then took a deep breath.

Then I headed in.

When I walked in, I began to take in the sights to get a feel for the place. A few seconds later, I heard my name called out. I looked to my left, and there she was at a table waiting on me. I noticed that she, too, was ten minutes early.

A girl who valued punctuality as much as I did. I was impressed.

As I approached the table, I could see that wonderful smile she smiled that accented her beauty.

Then I was there.

"Glad you could make it," she cheerily replied.

"I wouldn't miss it for the world," I said, sitting down.

There was a menu in front of me.

"This is a real nice place," I said, picking it up.

"I bet the food here is great," she said, looking over her menu.

We were silent for a moment, both trying to decide what we wanted.

While I looked at my menu, out of all of the thoughts that bombarded my mind at that time, the one question that lingered in the forefront of my mind above all was, What could this date lead to?

The possibilities were limitless.

Finally while still looking at her menu, she announced, "Oh this looks delicious. I think I'll have the chicken burrito with the side of refried beans and the side of rice."

"That sounds really good. I think I'll have the nachos platter."

Suddenly, a heavy-set, bald, older man, obviously a waiter, approached our table.

"Hi, my name is Floyd. I'll be your server today," he announced. "Can I get you any drinks?"

"Yes, I'll have Sprite," Sarah piped up.

"And I'll have Pepsi. And we're ready to place our order."

Floyd was writing down our drinks on his pad when he responded, "O.K., what can I get for you?"

I looked over to Sarah to let her know to place her order first. After she placed hers, I placed mine.

Floyd then replied, "I'll have those out shortly," and picked up our menus and left.

As soon as he was gone, I dove right into the conversation as I was eager to know all about her.

"So tell me about yourself," I replied.

"Well, I'm glad you asked," she said.

She seemed just as eager to tell me about herself as I wanted to hear.

"I was born in Montana and moved to Missouri to go to college. I got my nursing degree and then one day met my husband at a bakery I'd go to every morning."

I froze.

"Did you say your husband?" I nervously replied.

She then laughed and said, "Don't worry, we're not married anymore."

"Oh," I said with a sigh of relief. "What happened?"

"We got divorced."

Then Floyd came back with our drinks. He set them down in front of us and replied, "Your meals will be out shortly."

Then he was gone again.

"So tell me some things about you," Sarah said, sipping on her Sprite.

"Well, like you, I was married. But I met my wife in third grade."

The look of bafflement on Sarah's face made me laugh.

"Let me explain," I began. "We met in third grade and grew up together. We were childhood sweethearts. When we graduated from high school, we moved to Berkeley, CA., to live. Soon afterward, we decided to get married, and then we went on our honeymoon. Shortly, when we got back, I found out I had abdominal cancer."

"Oh no," Sarah announced in amazement.

"Oh, that's not the worst part. My sweet and loving wife, who I had grown up with and been with me all my life, suddenly tells me she's leaving me. And get this, for another man."

"What?! That's terrible."

"Yeah, that's what I said."

"Well, that just proves she didn't deserve you in the first place."

Suddenly, Floyd appeared with two large trays. He set mine in front of me and Sarah's in front of her.

"Enjoy," he replied and then turned and disappeared to the back area.

When he was gone, Sarah and I resumed our conversation. But we conversed on more lively and fun topics. We laughed and ate, and had an amazing time. When the meal was over, I paid the bill and gave Floyd a very generous tip. We then went to the parking lot, and I walked her to her car.

There I stood looking at her before finally announcing, "Well, I guess this is good night. I was just wondering if I could have..."

She then leaned forward and kissed me.

"A kiss?" she said, finishing my sentence for me.

"Yeah," I whispered.

Then we leaned in for another kiss.

There we were passionately kissing. This kiss went on for a while.

When we were done, I said, "Goodnight, Sarah," while looking in her eyes.

"Goodnight, William."

Then she turned and got in her car. I tapped on her window and she let it down.

"Can we go out again?" I asked.

"You have my number. Give me a call."

"Alright bye."

"Bye."

Then she drove off.

I got in my car too and drove off.

Chapter 35

Sarah and I went on more dates and spent more time with each other. We really enjoyed each other's company very much.

But what was all of this leading to?

One thing was for certain; we definitely had a solid relationship based on a liking for one another.

Today was Saturday, and we had plans to go see the new "Saw" movie at 7:15 p.m. I was in my room, lying down, staring at the ceiling, thinking about Sarah.

Then I started to get a nervous feeling in my stomach. But it was a good kind of nervousness.

The weather today was to be beautiful. A nice autumn day. Anna's birthday would be in two days.

So I decided to send her my prayers.

After a short prayer and acknowledgement to my first true love, I decided to go for a walk. I got up and grabbed my jacket and headed out.

When I got outside, I inhaled the sweet scent of autumn. As I walked, I took note of the changing trees. They were always so beautiful this time of season. The cool gusts of wind and the sweet air I inhaled filled my lungs and refreshed me as I thought only of positive thoughts for the future. After walking for a while, my head was clear as I began the journey back home.

When I got home, I opened the front door and stepped in. This is when I heard mom call out, "William, is that you? I'm in the kitchen, dear."

I walked to the kitchen to see mom sitting at the table with a cup of hot tea in her hand. At my spot at the table was a sandwich.

"I made you some lunch," she replied.

"Thanks, mom," I said and went to take my seat.

It was my favorite as a child and into adulthood – peanut butter and jelly.

I didn't waste any time indulging.

"So tell me about this girl Sarah, dear. You hardly talk about her."

"What's there to talk about? She's a real nice girl."

"Are you two serious about each other?"

"Yeah."

Suddenly mom began to yawn. "That's wonderful, honey," she replied. "I'm starting to feel a bit tired. I think I'd better take a nap."

"Alright, mom," I said, still eating my sandwich.

She then stood up, took her cup to the sink, and then sauntered out of the kitchen.

When I finished eating, I stood up and went back to my room to prepare for my date with Sarah.

Before long it was just about time to leave. I would be picking her up at her place. After I brushed my teeth and combed my hair, I put the cologne on, but not too much.

Then I was ready.

When I got to the living room, mom and dad were sitting on the couch.

"Bye, mom. Bye, dad. Don't wait up."

"Alright, have a good time," dad replied.

"Bye, honey. Show her your charm," mom announced.

"Alright," I said.

With that, I was gone.

As I drove, that same nervous feeling that I felt earlier came back.

In no time at all, I was there.

As I approached the front door, not only did I have that nervous feeling again, but now also my hands were sweaty.

What the hell's going on?

Then I rang her doorbell. A few seconds later, the door opened. And when it did, I beheld a beauty like never before.

"Hi Will."

"Hi Sarah."

I was waiting for the kiss when she announced, "Let's get going."

"Aren't you forgetting something?" I replied, leaning in for a kiss.

"Oh yes," she piped up and turned and went to her living room table.

"My purse."

Then she grabbed it and walked out past me – no kiss.

She knew I wanted a kiss, so this was her way of teasing me.

Then we got in the car and headed to Seville Theaters.

I was very excited on the way there because I so badly wanted to see this movie. Ever since I saw the previews for it, I was ever so anxious.

I was prepared for a treat.

When we got there, I parked and we went in. As soon as we got out of the car, I immediately took her hand. I wanted everyone to know we were a couple.

When we walked in, I saw there were lots of people. Some were children, some elderly, but lots of couples.

We went to the box office to purchase our tickets. Then we got popcorn and soda and were ready.

Our show was in theater twelve, so that's where we headed. We found our seats, and a few minutes later, the lights went low.

We watched the previews and then the show started. About twenty minutes into the show, I got that nervous feeling again. I then looked over at Sarah, who was looking at me. The gaze she had fixed upon me was a look I had never seen before.

Right then and there, I knew what that nervous feeling was. It was excitement – anticipation.

"Are you thinking what I'm thinking?" I asked her.

"Yeah, let's get out of here," she responded.

We got up, left the popcorn and soda there, and headed for the car.

When we got outside and to the car, before we got in, we kissed. It was passionate, sensual, and romantic all at once.

Then we got in the car and headed to her place.

While I drove, she placed her hand on my thigh. I tried to drive safely, but my hormones were jumping like crazy.

Finally, we were there.

We got out and kissed all the way up to the front door. We had to stop so she could get her keys and unlock the door. But once we were in, there was no stopping us. We made our way to the bedroom and closed the door.

Chapter 36

"Stop it," I replied, laughing while half-asleep and half-awake. I opened my eyes to see Sarah stroking my chest with her finger.

"Good morning, honey. I made you some breakfast," she whispered.

The good smells of sausage and eggs filled the house.

"Good morning," I replied and kissed her on the forehead.

We lay there for a little while longer, cuddled up in each other's arms. We both knew that there was no place else either of us wanted to be.

But we had to get up some time, so I pulled the cover back and sat up onto the bed. While I got dressed, she just layed there watching me. Then she too got up and got dressed. We went to the kitchen and had a hearty breakfast. While we ate, we talked and laughed, and the food was delicious.

When we were done, I grabbed my jacket and was about to leave.

There we stood at the front door.

Suddenly Sarah remarked, "You were amazing last night. You were like a wild beast."

I froze.

These were the exact same words Anna said to me after the first night we made love.

Sarah could see the strain on my face as she announced, "What's wrong? Was it something I said?"

"No," I said, coming back to reality.

I then kissed her and said, "I'll call you later. Bye."

"Bye."

Then I turned and left.

When I got home and walked in, there were mom and dad sitting on the couch. If I didn't know any better, I'd say they were there all night long.

So I asked them, "You weren't sitting here on the couch all night, were you?"

"No, of course not," dad piped up. We went to bed an hour after you left, woke up, and made breakfast."

"How was the movie, honey?" mom asked.

"I don't know. We didn't watch it all. Some time after it started, we left and went back to her place."

"That's my boy. And what did you do?" dad eagerly asked.

"Well, I'm not giving details, but you get the idea."

"He got that from me," dad proudly remarked to mom.

"And then she made me breakfast."

"And then?"

"And then that was it. I left."

"When's the next time you two will see each other again?" mom inquired.

"We didn't plan for that just yet. But I'll be calling her today so we can talk about it."

Suddenly, I looked over at mom, who had started sniffling and wiping her eyes.

"Mom, what's wrong?"

"I'm sorry for crying. It's just that you've come such a long way from Anna leaving you to beating cancer, and now you have this nice girl in your life. I'm so proud of you."

"Thanks, mom," I said with my eyes getting watery. "I couldn't have done it without you and dad."

"Well, William, I think you've got some reflecting to do because you certainly have come a long way," dad said.

"You're certainly right about that, dad. If you'll excuse me now, I'm going to call Sarah."

Then I turned and went to my room. When I got there, I layed on my bed and pulled my phone out. I dialed Sarah, and it rang twice before she answered.

"Hello."

"Hey Sarah."

"Oh hey, Will."

"What are you doing?"

"Just sitting here thinking about you."

"I've been thinking about you, too, about us. I have to ask, where did you learn to cook like that?"

When I was in high school, my dad was a chef, and he taught me how. So when do you want to get together again?"

"I was thinking maybe dinner tomorrow at "The Olive

Garden."

"Oh great. What time?"

"Around five or so."

"Sounds great. I'll see you tomorrow at five."

"Alright, babe. Bye."

"Bye."

When I ended the call with Sarah, I layed back and took dad's advice and reflected on my life. Then I thought of how it all came to this moment. Tomorrow will be the most important time of my life when I meet with Sarah.

I had a great feeling her answer would be, "Yes."

Chapter 37

Here I was at Starbuck's sitting at a table to myself enjoying a latte. I had been here quite a while in deep thought. Whereas I knew I was ready, the question was, was she?

Then I thought to myself, maybe I'm moving too fast.

But I've already prayed on it and searched my soul.

I couldn't be more ready.

Whereas I was assured on my part, this was the positive aspect. The negative aspect was what if, for some reason, she didn't feel the same or was not ready. This negative factor over-shadowed the positive, and just the mere idea of it, put me in a gloom state.

Finally, after much contemplation, I got up and left. I decided that if there was any moping to be done, it should be at home.

When I got home, I slumped down on the couch. After sitting there for about ten minutes, I began to realize how drained negative thinking can make you feel.

The next thing I knew, I was sitting on a blanket under a tree with Sarah. We were talking when suddenly two young children ran up to us.

"You guys tired yet?" I said to them.

"Yeah," they both simultaneously said.

"Alright, I'm ready if you are," I said, directing my attention to Sarah.

"Yeah, let's go," she answered while standing up.

Sarah and I held hands and walked, assuming the children were following close behind.

I looked back, and they were quite a distance back playing in the grass.

"Come on, Everett. Come on, Shelby," I announced. "We're going to Wendy's."

I slowly opened my eyes to see dad nudging my shoulder.

"Will, it's almost time for your date."

"What time is it?" I groggily responded.

"It's 4:16 p.m.," dad replied. "I decided to let you sleep a little longer. You appeared to be having a pretty good dream."

"Oh, it was wonderful."

"I'm sure it was. And I'm sure you'll tell me all about it later. But right now, you've got to get going."

I stood up and stretched.

"Am I ready to do this?" I thought to myself.

Of course I am.

Then I grabbed my jacket and headed out to meet Sarah at "The Olive Garden."

On the way there, that same negative idea of, "What if she says no," resurfaced.

Before I knew it, I was there.

I walked in and easily spotted her sitting at a booth – waiting on me.

Without any thought or rehearsal, I walked over to her with great strides and announced, "Sarah, I love you very much and I would be oh so glad if you'll accept my hand in marriage."

She sat there for a second before she started crying. This is when I got discouraged because I thought she would say, "No."

"Are you crying because you are saddened that I asked?"

"No, these are tears of joy. Yes, I will marry you."

Chapter 38

And so it happened for the second time. I stood at the altar and took vows to love and cherish my wife forever.

But this time, it was all too real.

The love in her heart she had for me was expressed when she recited her vows.

Then came the kiss.

As we kissed, I couldn't help but think to myself, "What was Anna doing right now at this moment?"

Then, just like that, it was over.

We had a wonderful reception and thanked everyone who showed up.

While we had a good time interacting with others, the only thing we wanted now was some alone time. As Sarah and I made the rounds personally thanking everyone for coming, we were both eager to spend our first night together as Mr. and Mrs.

Warner.

Sarah and I were by the punch bowl when she announced to me that she saw one of her old friends she had to catch up with.

As I watched Sarah walk away, I suddenly felt a hand on my shoulder.

"You did it," dad replied.

"Yeah, I did," I responded, still looking at Sarah.

"Your mom and I couldn't be more proud. You know, Will, there's been something I want to discuss with you."

"I'm listening."

"How do you feel about working in real estate? It just so happens I have a connection in the business, and I've already talked to the hiring manager. They could use an extra worker."

"Oh, dad, that's great!" I said, turning to hug him.

"But no pressure. Go see him when you're ready and once you get settled."

"Thanks, dad."

"Now, take Sarah and go have some fun. It's obvious you two want to be alone."

Then Sarah came up to me.

"Are you ready?" I said.

"Yeah."

"Thanks again, dad."

With that, we went to the car and drove on.

We were headed to the spot that overlooks the entire city. It was me and Anna's favorite hang out spot.

Chapter 39

Sarah and I moved in together into a wonderful home. Living life with her made me extremely happy. Just being with her every day gave me the warmest feeling.

Both her parents and my parents helped and supported us greatly.

And then I started working for Trent Bluford. I went to the interview, and he was very eager to hire me. The days I worked, I worked hard and diligently. Until after so much work and saving my money, and with what Sarah was making on her job, we were able to decorate our home real nice.

Today is Saturday, and Sarah is preparing a special meal for dinner.

I was in the living room sitting on the couch reading, "Tale of Henry Tinsdale" by James Mitchum Oates, while Sarah was in the kitchen cooking.

"Honey," she called out, "would you mind making a trip to

the store to get some oregano and garlic powder? I need it for tonight's dinner."

"Sure thing, babe," I responded.

I put my book marker on the page where I left off, grabbed my jacket, and headed out.

As I drove to the store, I began to hear my stomach growl.

It was time for a snack.

Then I was at the store.

When I walked in, I immediately went to aisle five to grab the oregano and garlic powder. No sooner than I got it and was headed to pay for it, did my stomach grumble again.

This is when I decided on a candy bar to ease my hunger. I went to the candy aisle and with so much candy there, the problem became which one did I want to choose.

But then it hit me.

Instead of buying junk food, why not have a healthy snack?

So with the oregano and garlic powder in hand, I made my way to the fruits and veggies aisle.

I began to search for a suitable snack.

"No, I don't want an orange, or an apple," I said to myself while looking.

"Ah, this'll do," I said, picking up a pear.

Suddenly, out of nowhere, I heard a voice say, "You know, the best pears are the softest ones because they're the ripest."

I then turned around to see Anna standing right behind me.

"Anna?" I whispered.

I could hardly recognize her. She looked pale and rundown.

"Hello, William," she replied.

I didn't know what to say.

Before me was the person who ruined my life and left me just when I needed her most.

Although instead of feeling anger, somehow I felt genuinely sorry for her.

"Hi," I finally said.

"How've you been?" she asked.

"I've been doing good. How about you?"

"Not so good. I have esophagus cancer and I'm expected to die soon."

Chapter 40

The natural reaction upon hearing this would've been shock. But for me, it was a flashback or remembrance of the first time I met Anna in third grade, and then up to this point. This is it – life as we know it.

"But I beat my cancer," I announced. "There's treatment that can actually make you cancer-free."

Anna then pulled off the wool hat from her head. I could see she was totally bald.

"I have tried chemotherapy and all other options. But the cancer was too aggressive."

"How much longer do you have?"

"They diagnosed me eight months ago and told me I had about eight months to live. So I'm expected to go any day now."

"What about your boyfriend, what's his name...?"

"Jeff."

"Yeah, what did he have to say?"

"He left me. He said the only thing I was good for was in bed, and he found someone else who could do that just fine. What about you? Have you moved on?"

"Yeah, I'm actually married now."

Then the tears began to stream down her face.

"Will, I want you to live life and be happy. I really do. But most of all, I want you to forgive me."

"I already have."

Then she turned and left out of my life forever – just as mysteriously as she'd come in.

I watched her walk away and disappear out of the store.

I then put the pear down I had in my hand. The hunger I had at first wasn't there anymore.

I went to the check-out line to pay for what I'd come for.

As I walked through the parking lot to the car, I suddenly had a shortness of breath. I was literally just now comprehending what just happened in the store.

I got in the car and sat there for a minute before the tears began rolling down my face.

"Dammit!" I shouted, slamming my hands against the steering wheel.

Then I started the car up and headed for home.

When I got home, I walked in and Sarah was still in the kitchen.

"What took so long?" she called out.

When I didn't answer, she called out, "Babe...,"

She then walked into the living room to see me sitting on the couch with my head buried in my hands, crying.

"Babe, what's wrong?" she said, rushing over to me.

"I saw Anna."

"What? Where?"

She was at the store, and she told me she has cancer and is expected to die any day now. It was horrible."

"Alright, slow down and tell me everything."

"She told me she has esophagus cancer and she took off her hat and didn't have any hair from the chemotherapy."

"Oh, Will," Sarah said, embracing me in a hug.

187

"The last thing she said to me was that she wanted me to forgive her. And I did. I forgave her a long time ago."

Chapter 41

The phone rang twice before mom answered.

"Hello."

"Hi, mom."

"Hi Will. Is everything alright? You don't sound so good."

"No," I somberly said. Then I began sobbing. "It was terrible. Just like out of a nightmare."

"Honey, slow down and tell me what it is."

"I saw Anna in the store today. She told me she has cancer and is expected to die any day now."

"Oh, that's horrible!"

"I admit I was pretty angry when she left me and the way she left me, but I never wanted anything like this to happen."

"Will, your father and I are here. Come over so we can talk about it."

"I think right now I just want to be alone."

"Alright, honey. Whenever you want to talk, we're here."

"Thanks, mom."

Then I hung up.

I looked to Sarah, who was sitting next to me. She then put her hand on my shoulder and soothingly replied, "I'm here for you."

I then looked into her eyes and pleadingly cried out, "Promise me you'll never leave me. No matter what."

"Will, you know I'm here for you."

"I need to hear you say it!" I shouted.

She leaned a little back from me. I could tell that me shouting at her frightened and startled her somewhat. I had never raised my voice at her before. She was quite surprised.

"Will...," she replied, placing her hand over her mouth.

"I'm sorry. I'm just so frustrated."

I could tell she was still a little uneasy by me showing aggression towards her.

"Babe, why don't you go on and finish dinner. I'll be there in a little bit."

"O.K.," she said, slowly standing up and going in the kitchen.

When she went in the kitchen, I stood up and went to the bedroom. When I got there, I closed the door and climbed in bed – clothes and shoes on.

I was tired.

Very tired.

I had no intention of eating dinner now, and Sarah knew it.

"You were my first, and I want you to be my last."

Upon hearing this, I hopped up in a cold sweat. These were the words Anna said to me on graduation night after we made love.

Then I looked over at Sarah, who was resting peacefully. Suddenly, my stomach began to growl. I was hungry from having missed dinner. I looked over at the clock on the nightstand, and it read 1:46 a.m. I decided to make my way to the kitchen. I slowly climbed out of bed so as not to wake Sarah. Once out of bed, I slowly walked to the door and then to the kitchen.

When I got there, I flipped the light on to see dishes in the sink.

"This isn't like her. Normally, she would've washed those," I thought to myself.

But I knew that like me, she was tired.

Everyone was tired.

I turned the kitchen light off and went to the living room to sleep on the couch so as not to bother my wife.

Chapter 42

An entire week rolled on, and here I was in this gloom and dismal state. It's now Friday morning when the phone rang.

"Hello," I answered.

"Hey, honey, do you have time to talk?" mom said.

"At the time, I'm actually a little busy," I lied.

"William, I think we definitely need to talk. And preferably face to face. There's someone here to see you."

My first and only notion of who this person might be is Anna.

"Alright, I'm on my way."

I hung the phone up, grabbed my jacket, and was out the door. I was in such a rush, I forgot to tell Sarah I was leaving. I got in the car and raced through traffic to get to my parents house.

When I got there, I walked right in to see mom and dad sitting on the couch, and right across from them were Anna's parents.

"Mom, dad, where's Anna?" I anxiously asked.

Then I looked over to Anna's mom, who, with tears in her eyes, announced, "She died two days ago."

Upon hearing this, everything fell silent to me. I couldn't hear or see anything around me. It was like I was in my own world. The only other time I had felt this way was when I found out that I was cancer-free and had beaten cancer.

When I finally came back to reality, I then realized the tears streaming down my face.

Then Anna's parents stood up, and my parents stood up and approached me. There we all embraced in one big hug.

Years have passed now, and Sarah and I have grown stronger and stronger together. We are now at a park and we are just now leaving. I look back at the two children playing in the grass and announce, "Come on, Everett. Come on, Shelby. We're headed to Wendy's."

Epilogue

The funeral for Anna was decent. A lot of people showed up to pay their respects. Sarah and I continued to grow together. We both thought it best that we start studying the Word more. We found a nice church to belong to and devoted our lives to serving God. Then Sarah encouraged me to pick back up on my dream of going to college. I was all in for it. She supported me greatly, and in no time at all, I walked across the stage and got my degree in Economics. At this time now, we have two children, Everett and Shelby. I have experienced a lot in my life – some good and some bad. All of which have shaped me into who I am today. Although I must say that in this time in my life is the best ever for me. But one thing is for certain, I never will forget my first true love – Anna.

Afterword

Years ago, when I was attending my second college, a month before graduation, I can remember feeling anxious and nervous. Both of these feelings were in a good way. I felt anxious because I couldn't wait to walk across the stage and receive the prize I awaited for and so justly deserved. But then I felt nervous because I couldn't guarantee, but could only hope that I would get a good job in my field of study and do lots of great things.

I can remember sitting in class, not focused on what the teacher was saying, because I was concentrated on planning my future and what that might hold. When suddenly my professor announced, "And now I'd like to introduce to you Mr. Benson Wright. Benson is a poet who has published a book of poems, and he would like to share some of his work with you and then tell you of his journey as a poet."

Suddenly, a young man came in, (about in his mid-twenties), and addressed the professor and the students in the class. He spoke for a little bit before starting on his first poem. As I listened, I became entranced with his words and the passion behind those words.

Finally, in the middle of his reciting, it hit me – I could become a poet. I listened to the tenure and good quality of his poems and then challenged myself to produce just as good as he! Once he was done, he took questions from the students. When there were no more questions, he thanked us for our time and left.

And here the yearning to create wonderful poetry had been started. The seed had been planted. I didn't waste any time. When I got home that night, I worked on and created my first poem which I entitled "The Origin of Poetry." I continued writing poems until I graduated. And then some time after that, I challenged myself again and said, "If I can write poems, it must not be much harder to write an actual book. Thus, I began working on my first book. However, after a few failed attempts in putting together my first book, I decided to write about something that I could easily and freely write about. I wrote my life story and got it published on Jan. 11, 2011.

And I've been writing ever since!

Ever since publishing my life story, it gave me the confidence and assurance that I could write a good quality book. So I continued writing more books. This book you are reading is currently my tenth book. In writing chapter twenty of this book, the poetry side of me called out, and I put together this neat little poem, which I entitled "Tying the Knot." I would greatly love to share this poem with you and a few others that I have written.

Tying the Knot

Here she is, my bride to be

Is the world moving slower, or is it just me

This angel is now in my life for the rest of my life

My friend, my companion, my love, my wife

The vows have been said and now here we start

To you, my queen, I open my heart

Here I stand looking deep into your eyes and into your soul
Searching

Our love is destined to be until the end

Because this is our 50th anniversary and we chose to get
married all over again

The Origin of Poetry

I can tell you now that you won't win, or know where to begin in your plights to find the origin of poetry

But what is real is the man behind the story

The origin of poetry comes from the last chapter of the Book of Life

For it is the story of eternal life

But you still ask what is the origin of poetry

To that, my answer is the origin of poetry comes from the greatest glory

Now that you know, ask that man in the mirror again

Because the origin of poetry comes from within

Floetry or Poetry

Is it floetry or poetry?

Floetry is the evil

Floetry is the hate

Floetry is the crime

Floetry is everything bad

With all of this said, I still do not know what floetry is

Poetry

Poetry is love

Poetry is beauty

Poetry is positive progression

With all of this said, I still do not know what poetry is

However, assuming that this is true, why is it that some poetry has sad meanings

The reason for this is floetry is poetry and poetry is floetry

Incarcerated

I cheat

I lie

I steal

I offend

Because I do not know where to begin

But I do know how it ends

I will end up dead at a very young age

But read on, do not turn the page

Because incarcerated in prison is not where I stand

But being incarcerated in society is where I am

The Graduate

The Graduate is who I am

I have done it

I have succeeded

I have made it in life

For now, the day is come when I take strife

I have walked the walk

And now I also can talk the talk

Because now I'm a graduate from a whole different aspect

From here it's up from the ghetto

And now I walk in my own shadow

Summary

William and Anna are childhood sweethearts. They grow up together through elementary school and then through high school. After graduating high school, their plans of going to college gets halted when William gets a visit from his cousin Joey. Joey's presence sets off a tension between William and Anna. Soon Anna and William move to California and later get married. But after the honeymoon, William gets some very bad news. Anna's reaction to this reveals who Anna really is. William then moves back home with his mom and dad and overcomes insurmountable odds. William finds another romance, and life is very good for him. But then one day he sees Anna in the store, and she tells him a horrific truth that is jaw-dropping.

www.ingramcontent.com/pod-product-compliance
Lightning Source LLC
Chambersburg PA
CBHW071732120626
46550CB00002B/492